The Boundary Waters Canoe Area

Volume 1: The Western Region

Robert Beymer

Wilderness Press
BERKELEY

An act pending in Congress when this book was printed would prohibit motorized boats on many lakes and streams where they are now allowed. Before deciding on your trip, inquire of Superior National Forest about the outcome of this proposed legislation. Write Superior National Forest, Box 338, Duluth MN 55801.

Copyright © 1978 by Robert Beymer
All rights reserved
Cover photo by J. Arnold Bolz
Maps by Jeff Schaffer
Design by Thomas Winnett

Library of Congress Card Catalog Number 77-88643
International Standard Book Number 911824-68-5

Printed in the United States of America
Published by Wilderness Press
        2440 Bancroft Way
        Berkeley CA 94704

Dedicated to Camp Northland

Where employment as a canoe trip guide gave me the opportunity to do much of the research necessary to write this book;

Where many a long-lasting friendship was made during the seven pleasant summers when it was my home; Whose spirit will be with me for the rest of my life!

Acknowledgments

A book like this one could never have been written without the help and encouragement of many people. I could never fully express my appreciation to all of those who had a part in its creation, but it is only fair to at least mention those who offered the greatest contributions.

Herb Evans, Director of the Voyageur Visitor Center in Ely, who supplied me with the U.S. Forest Service statistical data contained herein.

Earl Fisher, W.A. Fisher Company, who supplied the maps used for research.

Wally Schuette, Lowe Industries, who supplied the 17-foot Loweline canoe used for research during the Summer of 1977.

Richard A. Smith, Chuckwagon Foods, who supplied the trail food at discount for my research trips.

A.O. Berglund, Jr., Director of Camp Northland, and Skipper Berglund, founder of Camp Northland.

Anne Pomaranc, Betsy Crown and Jo Dunnick, who supplied many of the photographs used to illustrate my text.

Tim Bloom, Bill Donald, Fred Brown, Marty Danekind, Tim Nichols, Jeff Ryther and Tom Wilson — my associate guides at Camp Northland.

Jan Baker and Rex Miller — my expedition companions.

Gerald J. Beymer, who introduced me to the joys of camping experiences.

Ruth E. Beymer, who steadfastly encouraged me to write about those experiences.

Cheryl McFaul Beymer, who is my favorite canoeing companion.

Thomas Winnett, Editor-in-chief of Wilderness Press, for his faith in the success of this guide and his patience in dealing with me.

And all the good people with whom I have tripped into the BWCA and whom I have met on those excursions.

Bob Beymer
St. Paul, Minn.
February 20, 1978

Contents

Preface

This book is the result of my nine years of canoeing in the Boundary Waters Canoe Area. I was introduced to the BWCA in June 1967, along with 14 other members of my Explorer Post. Not a summer since then has gone by without at least one North Woods canoe trip, usually several.

Since my first summer as a guide in the Boundary Waters I have seen the need for a published trail guide, and as the number of visitors to this aquatic paradise has grown, the need has become even greater.

During the Summer of 1976, the US Forest Service implemented a new Visitor Distribution Program to "protect the water quality and other physical resources of the area and to assure that opportunities for a high quality wilderness experience are available to its users." Accordingly, from mid-May through Labor Day, daily limits have been established for the number of overnight permits that may be issued for each of the designated entry points.

With over a million pristine acres of lakes, rivers and forests within its borders, the BWCA is large enough to accommodate the present usage. So why do we need a quota system? Because, unfortunately, over two-thirds of the visitors to the BWCA use only 14 percent of the 73 designated entry points. The result is congestion on such popular lakes as Moose, Saganaga, Fall, Trout and Lake One.

It is my firm belief, however, that there would be no need for a quota system if canoeists only knew of the many entry points and routes available to them. Why would anyone want to paddle out of canoe "terminals" like Moose Lake when he could enter the Boundary Waters through the winding wilderness of Hog Creek, or the Kawishiwi River, or the Little Indian Sioux River?

This book is designed to help you discover a better way into the BWCA. It was written for the canoe camper who is capable of taking care of himself in a wilderness environment. It does not take you by the hand and lead you through the often complicated mazes of lakes and portages that characterize the BWCA. It does not always tell you when to turn right, when to turn left, or when to stop and take a picture. You should already possess the intelligence and understanding of the basic skills that are essential for a canoe trip into a wilderness, particularly the ability to guide yourself along the suggested routes without detailed directions. It does not include such topics as "what equipment you will need," or "how to plan your food," or "how to shoot a rapids," or "how to pack your gear." Many good "how to " books have been written about canoeing and camping. This guide is a "where to" book. If you need information about techniques, I suggest you read several of the "how to" books and pick out what is appropriate to your needs.

Bearse, Ray, *The Canoe Camper's Handbook*. New York: Winchester Press, 1944.

Boy Scouts of America, *Canoeing,* B.S.A. North Brunswick N.J.: B.S.A. 1968.

Hassenfuss, Joseph, *American Red Cross Canoeing Manual*. New York: Doubleday & Co., 1959.

Jacobson, Cliff, *Wilderness Canoeing and Camping*. New York: E.P. Dutton, 1977.

Riviere, Bill, *Pole, Paddle and Portage:* A Complete Guide to Canoeing. Boston: Little, Brown & Co., 1974.

Sandreuter, William O., *Whitewater Canoeing*. New York: Winchester Press, 1976.

To capture the mood of canoeing in the BWCA, read any of Sigurd F. Olson's vivid accounts: *Reflections from the North Country, The Hidden Forest, Wilderness Days, Open Horizons, Runes of the North, The Lonely Land, Listening Point, The Singing Wilderness*.

This is a *comprehensive* guide, including all entry points that are useful to canoeists in the western half of the Boundary Waters Canoe Area, from Crane Lake east to Kawishiwi Lake. A future volume will take over where this one leaves off, dealing with the entry points in the eastern half of the BWCA.

Ch. 1:
Introduction to the BWCA

The Boundary Waters Canoe Area is paradise for the wilderness canoeist. Stretching for 200 miles along the Canadian border of northeastern Minnesota, this magnificent wilderness offers over 1,200 miles of canoe routes through some of the most beautiful country in the world. That's why over 125,000 persons visit it each year. At over a million acres, it is the second largest unit of our National Wilderness Preservation system, containing the largest virgin forests remaining east of the Rocky Mountains.

HISTORY

The canoe routes on which you will paddle are the very same ones used for hundreds of years by the Sioux and Chippewa Indians and by the French-Canadian Voyageurs. Jacques De Noyons, in about 1688, was probably the first white man to paddle through the lakes and streams that now compose the BWCA. At that time, the Sioux may have still been the dominant Indians in the area. But by the time of the first fur traders in the 18th Century, the Chippewas had moved into the region from the east and had driven the Sioux farther west onto the plains. From then to about 1800, French-Canadian Voyageurs paddled their birch-bark canoes from the hinterlands of northwestern Canada to the shores of Lake Superior, transporting furs from trappers toward the European markets.

During the latter half of the 19th Century, settlers moved into the area, including farmers, loggers and miners. After the railroad penetrated the area, extensive logging and mining operations threatened to devastate the entire region.

The Superior National Forest was designated in 1909, and within it, in 1926, one thousand acres were set aside as a primitive roadless area. This area was enlarged in the 1930's and in 1939 the wilderness area was redesignated the Superior Roadless Primitive Area, establishing the present boundaries containing over one million acres. In 1958, the current name was adopted. The BWCA is regulated by the Secretary of Agriculture and is administered by the U.S. Forest Service.

Thanks to the efforts of conservationists throughout the years, this beautiful region looks almost the same today as it did when De Noyons first viewed it.

WILDLIFE

Nothing represents the Boundary Waters better than the eerie "laughter" of the loon, the Minnesota State Bird. But many other birds are equally at home here, including the bald eagle, the gull, the great blue heron, and the Canadian jay. In the BWCA you will also find the last substantial population of timber wolves in the "lower forty-eight," as well as a large population of moose, white-tailed deer, black bear, beaver and fox. Other mammals include the lynx, fisher, mink, muskrat, otter, marten, weasel, coyote, and a variety of squirrels.

The predominant game fish are northern pike, walleye, smallmouth bass and lake trout. Crappies and bluegill are also plentiful in some of the lakes. Even rainbow and brook trout have been stocked in some lakes.

The North Woods are covered largely by a coniferous forest, made up of jack pine, Norway pine, white pine, tamarack, black spruce, white spruce, balsam fir and white cedar. There are also extensive stands of deciduous trees, including paper birch and quaking aspen. Very few land areas in the BWCA are not forested.

BEARS

Black bears are common throughout the BWCA. Although they are not considered to be dangerous and are usually quite shy around campers, they may be pests when searching for food — your food.

Over the years they have learned that canoe campers always travel with food packs. And where campers are most frequently found camping, the bears are most frequently a problem. An unpleasant encounter with a bear could bring an abrupt end to your canoe trip. With a few precautions, how-

ever, you will have no problem with these interesting creatures.

1) Never keep food in your tent.

2) Always keep your distance from bear cubs. They may
look very cute, but their mother is very protective and probably close by.

3) Never corner a bear. If left with no alternatives, a bear,
like any other animal, may turn belligerent.

4) If a bear does happen into your campsite, make noise by
yelling or banging pots and pans together. If this is not
enough, throwing rocks at it may do the trick.

5) When you are away from your campsite, and at night,
hang your food above the ground and *away* from tree trunks.
Remember that a bear can climb a tree, so the food must be a
safe distance (about 6 feet) away from the trunk and from any
limbs large enough to support a bear's weight.

CLIMATE

In northern Minnesota, spring, summer and fall are
crowded into a span of about five months — May through
September. Perhaps the best seasons for canoeing in the
Boundary Waters are spring (May) and autumn (September).
At those times, water levels are usually the highest and in-
sects are usually the least bothersome. Fishing is also the best
at these times. But those months are also, normally, the
coolest times of the canoeing season. Early June and late
August to mid-September are usually the wettest periods.

July and early August normally offer the best weather for
campers. But, because that is a dry time, water levels of some
streams may be too low for navigating a loaded canoe,
eliminating many excellent route possibilities.

Temperatures and rainfall vary, of course, throughout
the BWCA. The following statistics, recorded in International
Falls, represent approximations for the western half of the
BWCA.

	May	June	July	Aug.	Sept.
Average temperature	51°	60°	66°	63°	53°
Average low each day	38°	48°	53°	51°	41°
Average high each day	63°	72°	78°	76°	64°
Precipitation	2.6"	3.9"	3.5"	3.6"	2.9"

A WILDERNESS?

There are those purists who would not classify the BWCA as a true wilderness. In one sense, they are right. Regulations dictate that you must camp only in Forest Service campsites, which are equipped with stationary fire grates and box latrines. There are obvious signs all around you that other people have camped at that very same spot many, many times before.

There are also those who declare that you must paddle for weeks before you can truly feel a sensation of "wilderness." Regarding the BWCA, I must disagree. Seldom are more than one or two long portages necessary for the BWCA visitor to perceive the true wilderness around him. The disquieting drone of motors fades into the past, and one enters a new world of only natural sensations. Depending on your point of entry, it could take a day, or maybe two, to find your wilderness. On the other hand, it may be waiting only minutes from your launching site, scarcely more than a stone's throw away from road's end. Wherever you start, a magnificent wilderness is not far away in the BWCA.

Ch. 2:
How to Use This Guide

This book is an accumulation of *suggestions*. It does not give all possible routes into the BWCA. Quite the contrary, the routes that you could take are virtually infinite in number. Furthermore, you may wish to follow only a part of one route, or you may wish to combine two or more routes. All of the routes suggested are "round trip" — they begin and end at (or within walking distance of) the same location. There is no need for car shuttles between two points.

Any group entering the Boundary Waters must have in its possession a travel permit, granting permission to enter through one of the 73 designated entry points. Since this guide treats only the western half of the Boundary Waters, and since not all entry points are well suited for canoeists, only 24 entry points are discussed in this book:

1	Trout Lake	23	Range River
4	Crab Lake	24	Fall Lake
6	Slim Lake	25	Moose Lake
7	Big Lake	26	Wood Lake
8	Big Moose Lake	27	Snowbank Lake
9	Sioux River (South)	30	Lake One
12	Little Vermilion Lake	31	Farm Lake
14	Sioux River (North)	32	South Kawishiwi River
16	Moose River	34	Island River
19	Stuart River	35	Isabella River
21	Fourtown Lake	36	Hog Creek
22	Horse Lake	37	Kawishiwi Lake

Seventeen other entry points exist in the western half of the Boundary Waters, but they are not included in this guide for the following reasons.

Some are used mostly by hikers.

3	Pine Lake Trail	13	Little Vermilion Trail
10	Norway Trail	15	Sioux Hustler Trail

18   Lac La Croix Trail   28   Kekekabic Trail
20   Angleworm Trail

Some are grouped with other entry points that are included in the guide, because the Government has grouped them for the purpose of quota restrictions.

 2   Phantom Lake (with Crab Lake)
 5   Cummings Lake (with Crab Lake)
11   Blandin Road (with the Moose River)
17   Portage River (with the Moose River)
29   North Kawishiwi River (with the South Kawishiwi River)
33   Nickel Creek (with the South Kawishiwi River)
63   Four Mile Portage (with Fall Lake)

Some are from Canada.

71   From Canada into lakes east of Basswood Lake
72   From Canada into Basswood Lake
73   From Canada into lakes west of Basswood Lake

The routes included in this guide are then grouped according to accessibility: 1) those accessible from the Echo Trail, 2) those accessible from the Fernberg Road, and 3) those accessible from State Highway 1.

Using statistical data and personal observations, each entry point is briefly discussed. Statistics given pertain to the Summer of 1976, the most current data available when this book went to press.

1) **Permits:** The estimated number of travel permits used to groups using the entry point in 1977, including all modes of transportation.

2) **Popularity Rank:** The relative popularity of the entry point, compared with all other entry points (73 total) with all other entry points (73 total).

3) **Daily Quota:** The maximum number of overnight travel permits that can be issued each day to groups using the entry point.

Further discussion includes the entry point's location (airline distance from Ely), how to get there, public campgrounds nearby, amount of motorized use through the entry point, and other comments of interest to canoeists.

Following the discussion of an entry point are the suggested routes that use that entry point. Introductory remarks will tell you: 1) how many days to allows; 2) the approximate number of miles; 3) the number of different lakes, rivers and creeks to be encountered, as well as the number of portages en route; 4) the difficulty (easy, challenging or rugged), based largely on the frequency, length and difficulty of portages; 5) Fisher maps that cover the route; and 6) general comments, including fishing opportunities. Then each route is broken down into suggested days, giving the sequence of lakes, streams and portages, followed by points of special interest.

Example: DAY 2: **Little Trout Lake,** p. (portage) 376 rods, **Little Indian Sioux River,** p. 40 rods, **river,** p. 35 rods, **river,** p. 20 rods, **river,** p. 120 rods, **Otter Lake,** p. 5 rods, **Cummings Lake.**

Explanation: On the hypothetical second day of this route, you will paddle across Little Trout Lake, and portage 376 rods to the Little Indian Sioux River. You will follow the river to Otter Lake, negotiating four portages along the way. Finally, you will portage 5 rods from Otter Lake to Cummings Lake and make camp there, at one of the campsites marked by a red dot on the Fisher map.

A word about the use of rods: One rod equals 16½ feet. Since this is roughly the length of most canoes, it is the unit of linear measurement used in canoe country. The Forest Service has posted wood signs indicating the number of rods at the beginnings of most portage trails in the BWCA, and the Fisher maps also use this unit of measurement. Because these maps are not topographic, however, the indicated number of rods tells you little about the difficulty of the portages to be encountered. Long ones may be quite easy, and short ones may be extremely tough. This guide will warn you about the tough ones.

Of course, any route may be made more difficult by completing it in fewer days than recommended, or made easier by adding days. If you plan to do a great deal of fishing, you should probably add at least one day for each three days suggested. For longer trips, you may also want to add layover days to your schedule, in the event that wind, foul weather, sickness or injury should slow you down. (Always carry an extra day's supply of food too, for just that reason.)

MAPS

It would be nearly impossible to show detailed maps on the pages of this book. Instead, you will a find foldout map of

the entire western region inside the back cover. When taking
your trip, however, I recommend the waterproof-parchment
maps published by the W.A. Fisher Company. Fifteen
"Superior-Quetico Maps" combine to cover all the Boundary
Waters Canoe Area and Canada's Quetico Provincial Park, as
well as the rest of the Canadian border from International
Falls to Lake Superior. Campsites are updated annually on
these maps which are designed specifically for the canoeist
and the fisherman. The campsites are indicated by red dots on
the maps.

The discussion of each route tells you which maps cover it.
You can order them from:

W.A. Fisher Company
Box 1107
Virginia, MN 55792

They cost 50c each, plus 4% sales tax, plus a shipping charge of
35c for three maps and 5c for each additional map. Or you can
buy your maps when you arrive in northern Minnesota from
any one of many canoe-trip outfitters.

OBTAINING TRAVEL PERMITS

A 100% long-term reservation system is in use. All overnight travel permits are available through advance reservations. You do not have to make a reservation before arriv-
ing at the BWCA, but it is advisable, since quotas at some
entry points fill up early.

A reservation allows a party to obtain one travel permit
for entry into the BWCA *on* the starting date and *at* the entry
point specified on the reservation. Reservation requests must
include the following: 1) the entry-point number (or lake
name), 2) the starting date, and 3) name and address of the
applicant, and 4) name of one other group member. Alternate
starting dates and entry points may be listed on the applica-
tion in case the first choice is not available.

The daily limits are based on the number of campsites on
the routes served by each entry point, and they vary considerably from one entry point to another. The daily entry
limits established for each entry point do not apply for day use,
for which there is no limit.

The distribution of permits begins on the Thursday pre-
ceding the opening weekend of the Minnesota fishing season
(usually around mid May) and ends on Labor Day. There are

no limits on the number of overnight permits issued before or after these dates.

Reservations may be made by mail, telephone or personal visit to the Forest Service office administering the entry point where your trip will start. Reservations sent by mail, however, must be received not later than 14 days before the starting day. Reservations by telephone call and personal visit may be made as late as the day of entry.

Permits will not be sent through the mail. They must be claimed by the applicant at the Forest Service permit-issuing station that has jurisdiction over the entry point, by 10 a.m. of the departure day. Unclaimed reservations will be given out to others on a first-come, first-served basis, one to a user, after 10 a.m. of the departure day.

Different "control stations" are assigned to different entry points. Make your reservation requests accordingly:

Entry Points	Control Station	Address	Telephone #
1,9,12,14,16	La Croix Ranger Stn. Cook, MN 55723	Box 1085,	(218) 666-5421
4,6,7,8,14,16,19, 21-33	Voyageur Visitor Ctr. Ely, MN 55731	Box 149,	(218) 365-6126
34 & 35	Isabella Ranger Stn. Isabella, MN 55607	Box 207,	(218) 293-4255
36 & 37	Tofte Ranger Stn. Tofte, MN 55615		(218) 663-7280

HEAVY USE PERIODS

When planning your trip, you may increase your chance of obtaining a BWCA permit by considering the following guidelines.
1. The busiest days for entry are Saturday, Sunday and Monday. You will have a better chance on one of the other four days of the week.
2. Memorial Day weekend, Independence Day weekend, Labor Day weekend and the first three weeks of August are the busiest times.
3. Consider using an entry point that has, in the past, ranked low in popularity. A majority of visitors use a very small minority of the entry points.

RULES AND REGULATIONS

The following regulations apply to all users of the BWCA.

1. Party size is limited to 10 people. No more than 10 may use a campsite at one time.
2. Camping is permitted only at Forest Service campsites that have steel fire grates and box latrines.
3. Open campfires are permitted only within constructed fireplaces at developed campsites.
4. Nonburnable, disposable food and beverage containers are not permitted.
5. Camping is limited to a maximum of 14 consecutive days at one campsite.
6. Fires must be drowned with water and be dead out before a campsite may be vacated.
7. Entry to the BWCA must be made at the entry point, and on the date shown on the travel permit.
8. It is unlawful to cut live trees, shrubs or boughs.
9. Motorized travel and mechanical portaging are permitted only on certain specified routes.
10. No watercraft, motor, mechanical device or equipment not used in connection with the current visit may be stored on or moored to National Forest land and left unattended.
11. No motorized or mechanical equipment of any type is permitted within the BWCA, except as specified above.
12. The use of firearms is discouraged.
13. Use cord instead of nail and wire.
14. Obey all state and local laws and regulations.

A FINAL WORD

Believe it or not, these age-old routes *do change*. In fact, they may change several times each year. A rock-strewn rapids that requires a portage in mid-August may be a navigable channel three weeks later, after the autumn rains. A portage indicated as 15 rods on the map may turn out to be 35 rods in reality, when the water level is so low that you must walk an extra 20 rods before the water is deep enough to set your canoe down. When a portage becomes too eroded from over-use, the Forest Service sometimes constructs a new one, which is usually longer than the original. And, occasionally, an author's memory and notes fail him and a mistake is made. So if you have any comments, suggestions or corrections to make pertaining to this guide, please write the author (in care of the publisher). Thank you.

Ch. 3:
Entry from the Echo Trail

The Western Region

The western region of the Boundary Waters Canoe Area contains most of the entry points included in this guide. Twelve entry points are easily accessible from the Echo Trail. Another entry point (#1-Trout Lake) is most easily accessible from State Highway 1-169, but because of its proximity to the other entry points in the western region, it fits much better in this category than with the other entry points accessible from State Highway 1, which are southeast of Ely.

The Echo Trail is a winding, hilly, scenic drive that most people find delightful, if they don't have to drive it every day. To get to it from the Voyageur Visitor Center east of Ely, drive ½ mile east on State Highway 169 to its junction with County Road 88. Turn left here and follow this new, good highway for 2½ miles to its junction with County Road 116, which is commonly called the Echo Trail.

The Echo Trail winds its way north and west for about 45 miles to County Road 24, near Echo Lake and south of Little Vermilion Lake (#12), the westernmost entry point for the Boundary Waters. The road surface is blacktop for the first 8½ miles, but it is gravel the rest of the way. It does straighten out, however, near the Moose River entry point, and from there on it is not a bad gravel road. Most of the "trail" is treacherous, though, so drive with care.

Entry Point 1 —Trout Lake

Permits: 1840
Popularity Rank: 7
Daily Quota: 18

Location: Trout Lake is accessible from Lake Vermilion, about 15 airline miles due west of Ely. From Ely follow State Highway 1-169 west for 26 miles to the junction of 1-169 and County Road 77, about four miles west of Tower, Minnesota. Turn right on County Road 77 and follow it northwest for 11 miles to the public landing on Moccasin Point.

Description: Public campgrounds on or near Lake Vermilion's south shore are located at Tower-Soudan State Park, McKinley Park and Tower Park. Any of these will provide you with a convenient place to spend the night prior to the canoe trip. All are less than twenty miles from the public access on Vermilion.

Lake Vermilion is a very popular and well-populated lake. It is particularly attractive to aquatic motorists, many of whom travel into Trout Lake and the adjacent lakes of Pine, Little Trout and Oriniack. Of all entry points into the BWCA, Trout Lake boasts the highest percentage of motor boats and the lowest percentage of canoes without motors. Of the 1840 permits issued to groups entering Trout Lake in 1977, only 118 went to canoes without motors — a mere 7 % of the total use, and only 6% of the summer use. Since motors are restricted to Trout and its three neighboring lakes, and since Trout Lake is the sixth most heavily used entry point for the BWCA, this all means that you will find a great deal of congestion, mostly in the form of motorboats, in the IMMEDIATE vicinity of Trout Lake.

Nevertheless, it also means that very few permits are issued to groups that can penetrate the lakes and rivers beyond the immediate vicinity. The conclusion: you can quickly pass through one of the busiest and noisiest lakes in the Boundary Waters and into one of the least traveled and most pristine areas within the BWCA, offering as much solitude and bountiful wildlife as you should ever hope to encounter. If you can tolerate the first and last days, you will surely find a wilderness trip from this entry point to be outstanding.

Route #1: The Cummings Lake Loop

4 Days, 47 Miles, 14 Lakes, 1 River, 5 Creeks, 22 Portages
Difficulty: Rugged
Fisher Maps: 111, 112

Introduction: This route will take you from Lake Vermilion north through Trout and Little Trout lakes to the lengthy portage into the Little Indian Sioux River. You will paddle east up this tiny, winding stream, through marshy terrain teeming with wildlife, to its headwaters from Otter and Cummings lakes. From the east end of Cummings Lake, you will turn south and then west, navigating the tiny lakes and streams that will return you to the busy motor route from which you began.

Your first and last days will probably be shared with many others, but solitude will be yours to cherish in the remote eastern portion of this interesting loop. Moose and deer are plentiful along the Little Indian Sioux River, and fishing is good in many of the lakes along the route. Try for northern pike or bass in Cummings, Otter, Little Trout and Trout lakes. Or catch a breakfast of walleye from Chad, Buck, Little Trout or Trout lakes. And, by all means, don't forget the NAME of your entry point; there are lake trout to be found in the depths of Trout Lake.

DAY 1: **Lake Vermilion,** p. 60 rods, **Trout Lake, Little Trout Creek, Little Trout Lake.** Your first day won't be too exciting, unless you are run over by a motorboat, or unless a strong northwest wind makes crossing Trout Lake very difficult or impossible. (If the latter is the case, I suggest you reverse this route and portage 260 rods into Pine Lake. You will bypass the main portion of Trout Lake, and a west wind will be no problem until you reach Cummings Lake and begin your journey back to Trout Lake.) Even if you arrive at Little Trout Lake early in the day, I suggest you stop there and make camp. There are no designated USFS campsites on the Little Indian Sioux River, and very few places that could even be MADE into campsites.

DAY 2: **Little Trout Lake,** p. 376 rods, **Little Indian Sioux River,** p. 40 rods, **river,** p. 35 rods, **river,** p. 20 rods, **river,** p. 30 rods, **river,** p. 40 rods, **river,** p. 20 rods, **river,** p. 28 rods, **river,** p. 120 rods, **Otter Lake,** p. 5 rods, **Cummings Lake.** You will find this day to be a sharp contrast from the prior day of paddling on big lakes. With seven short portages scattered along the meandering Sioux River, travel is deceivingly slow. Relax and enjoy the bountiful wildlife and absence of other canoes along its course. I once witnessed six deer and a cow moose leisurely drinking from the river's swampy bank. Who knows how many other creatures watched US paddle silently through this winding wilderness? The 376-rod portage from Little Trout Lake to the river is not well traveled and may be muddy. But there are no major inclines over which to pass. Several nice campsites are near the east end of Cummings Lake.

DAY 3: **Cummings Lake,** p. 35 rods, **Korb Creek, Korb Lake, Korb Creek,** p. 1-3 rods, **creek, Little Crab Lake, Lunetta Creek, Lunetta Lake,** p. 60 rods, **Lunetta Creek,** p. 100 rods, **Schlamm Lake,** p. 210 rods, **Glenmore Lake,** p. 195 rods, **Western Lake,** p. 80 rods, **Buck Lake,** p. 250 rods, **Chad Lake.** It is primarily because of this day that this route is labeled "rugged." You will be carrying your load across eight portages totalling over 850 rods, four of which are well over half a mile each! None are difficult, however, just long. Should you wish to get back to Trout Lake sooner, a good short-cut is possible by portaging 480 rods from Cummings Lake directly into Buck Lake. This trail is virtually flat, and there are sixteen canoe rests along the way. But this will eliminate a very scenic series of small lakes and streams between Cummings and Schlamm lakes. Chad is known as a good walleye lake, so eat well! On the 250-rod portage between Buck and Chad lakes, notice how the interconnecting stream changes directions midway across the portage.

DAY4: **Chad Lake,** p. 260 rods, **Pine Creek, Pine Lake,** p. 260 rods, **Trout Lake,** p. 60 rods, **Lake Vermilion.** Your first 260-rod portage gradually ascends 83 feet from the shore of Chad Lake before dropping steeply to Pine Creek. The second is similar, climbing 92 feet above Pine Lake before descending steeply to the shore of Trout Lake. Once again, you will now be back on the heavily traveled motor route from whence you came.

Route #2: The Winding Rivers Route

7 Days, 88 Miles, 17 Lakes, 4 Rivers, 2 Creeks, 33 Portages
Difficulty: Rugged
Fisher Maps: 107, 111, 112

Introduction: This strenuous route will take you north from Lake Vermilion through Trout and Little Trout lakes and north down the meandering Little Indian Sioux River, across the Echo Trail to the Pauness lakes. From Lower Pauness you will paddle and portage east through the Shell chain of lakes to Oyster Lake. Then you will turn south and re-enter the unique world of small rivers, as you paddle down the Oyster River and up the Nina-Moose and Moose rivers, across the Echo Trail, to Big Moose Lake. With river travel behind you, you will now work your way (and I mean WORK) through the tranquil lakes and long portages leading back to Trout and Vermilion lakes. Nearly half of your route will be on small, winding rivers. Most of the other half will be on portages, the last five totalling 1,830 rods, or an average of 366 RODS EACH! Nine of your portages will be in excess of 200 rods, the longest nearly two miles. It all adds up to a route that I call RUGGED.

If portaging does not scare you and rivers "turn you on," you will surely find this loop delightful. The portions of the Little Indian Sioux and Moose rivers that lie north of the Echo Trail are rather heavily traveled at times. They are among the 15 most popular entry points for the BWCA, and motors are permitted on both. But the lakes between them are off limits to motorized craft, as are the upper portions of both rivers (south of the Echo Trail). The region between Trout Lake and the Echo Trail is used much less than the northern sector, and you will find no one but dedicated wilderness enthusiasts here.

DAY 1: **Lake Vermilion,** p. 60 rods, **Trout Lake, Little Trout Creek, Little Trout Lake.** If strong westerly winds prohibit navigation across Trout Lake, an alternate route bypasses the main portion of this huge lake: portage 260 rods into Pine Lake, and follow Pine Creek around to the 40-rod portage back into the northeast corner of Trout. This will obviously take longer. Regardless of the time, however, you should go no farther than Little Trout Lake, as there are no designated campsites on the Little Indian Sioux River.

DAY 2: **Little Trout Lake,** p. 376 rods, **Little Indian Sioux River,** p. 20 rods, **river,** p. 120 rods, **river,** p. 8 rods, **river,** p. 120 rods, **river,** p. 60 rods, **river, Upper Pauness Lake.** This will be a long day of paddling down the gradually widening, deepening and straightening channel of the Little Indian Sioux River. Between portages it is virtually impossible to know EXACTLY where you are. Use the portages as landmarks, and alert yourself to the GENERAL direction of travel. Watch out for traffic as you cross the Echo Trail at the 120-rod portage. From that point on, the number of canoes you will see will greatly increase, and motors are permitted. You will be wise to claim the first campsite you see on Upper Pauness Lake.

DAY 3: **Upper Pauness Lake,** p. 8 rods, **Lower Pau-**

ness Lake, p. 216 rods, **Shell Lake,** p. 10 rods, **Little Shell Lake,** p. 4 rods, **Lynx Lake,** p. 280 rods, **Ruby Lake,** p. 10 rods, **Hustler Lake,** p. 240 rods, **Oyster Lake.** When your trip is over, you may look back at this day as one of the roughest. Of the three portages over 200 rods, though, only one is really wicked. The 216-rod trail from Lower Pauness Lake to Shell Lake is merely long, and not too steep. It intersects the Sioux-Hustler Foot Trail. The 280-rod path from Lynx Lake to Ruby Lake, on the other hand, climbs steeply to an elevation 128 feet above Lynx before gradually descending 72 feet to Ruby Lake. And, alas, the trail from Hustler Lake to Oyster Lake is mostly downhill; after gaining 64 feet across a third of the portage, it then descends 141 feet throughout the last half mile to Oyster Lake. Take time at the beginning of this day to paddle to the northwest end of Lower Pauness Lake and hike down into the scenic granite gorge through which Devil's Cascade plunges toward Loon Lake.

DAY 4: **Oyster Lake,** p. 60 rods, **Oyster River,** p. 20 rods, **Oyster River, Nina-Moose River,** p. 96 rods, **river,** p. 70 rods, **river, Nina-Moose Lake.** This day is intended to be short and easy. Nina-Moose is far from being the most scenic lake in the North Woods, but there are no designated USFS campsites beyond it until you reach Big Moose Lake, nine portages and a lot of winding river away. Pick a campsite early, as this is on a heavily used motor route, and relax while fishing for some of the northern pike, walleye or bass that inhabit this shallow lake. Along the western shoreline, you will see evidence of the 1971 forest fire that scourged nearly 25 square miles of woodland between here and the Little Indian Sioux River.

DAY 5: **Nina-Moose Lake, Moose River,** p. 25 rods, **river,** p. 20 rods, **river,** p. 160 rods, **river,** p. 77 rods, **river,** p. 40 rods, **river,** p. 40 rods, **river,** p. 17 rods, **river,** p. 160 rods, **river,** p. 60 rods, **Big Moose Lake.** The Moose River is another narrow, winding little stream through marshy terrain. Almost choked with vegetation during prime summer months, visibility along your route is frequently hardly more than a few yards in front of the canoe. Travel is slow, as you paddle against the current and meander considerably. Big Moose Lake is most impressive after a full day on this tiny stream. You should have little or no competition for the four campsites here.

DAY 6: **Big Moose Lake,** p. 580 rods, **Cummings Lake,** p. 480 rods, **Buck Lake,** p. 250 rods, **Chad Lake.** Your first trek of the day (and longest of the whole trip) crosses several small hills at both ends, but the major portion of the path follows a nearly level ridgetop. Hiking is quite easy, and there are 19 canoe rests along the way. The next 1½-mile portage is even more level, with 16 canoe rests at regular intervals along the path. The third portage will seem like nothing after the first two, although it does gently surmount a 50-foot hill. Notice how the stream between Chad and Buck lakes changes direction midway across the portage.

DAY 7: **Chad Lake,** p. 260 rods, **Pine Creek, Pine Lake,** p. 260 rods, **Trout Lake,** p. 60 rods, **Lake Vermilion.** Your first 260-rod carry gradually ascends 83 feet from the shore of Chad Lake before dropping steeply to Pine Creek. The second is similar, climbing 92 feet above Pine Lake before descending steeply to the shore of Trout Lake.

Entry Point 4—Crab Lake

Permits: 317
Popularity Rank: 26
Daily Quota: 5

Location: Crab Lake is accessible from big Burntside Lake, a very popular and populated lake located about 4 miles northwest of Ely. Several public accesses are situated around Burntside, of which two are the most practical for the suggested routes. SOUTH SHORE: from a junction on Highway 1-169 about 3 miles west of Ely, drive north on County Road 88 3 miles to the public access road (just west of Burntside Lodge). Or, from the southeast end of the Echo Trail, follow County Road 88 5 miles west to Burntside Lake. NORTH ARM: Follow the Echo Trail (Co. Rd. 116) north and west from County Road 88 for 9 miles. Turn left onto County Road 644, and follow this winding gravel road southwest for 2 miles to the public access on the left (and the Slim Lake portage on the right). You will find this located just past the entrance to YMCA Camp Widjiwagan.

Description: Camping is prohibited at both accesses. Fenske Lake Campground, located just 3 miles from the North Arm access on the Echo Trail (toward Ely) is a good place to camp the night before departing from the North Arm access. It takes about a 20-minute drive to reach the South Shore access from this campground.

Although Burntside is a lake laden with motor boats, motors are prohibited through the Crab Lake Entry point. Even if they were legal, I doubt that many would enter, as it requires crossing a one-mile uphill portage. In spite of its length, this portage is actually quite easy, following a wide, smooth path that ascends only about 100 feet. Eleven canoe rests are situated evenly along this gentle slope.

Nevertheless, not too many canoeists enter the BWCA this way. Consequently, Crab Lake provides one of the quickest escapes into solitude of any BWCA entry point. Here you can "easily" retreat for a three-day weekend and see few, if any, people beyond Crab Lake itself.

The Phantom Lake entry point (#2) and the Cummings Lake Trail (#5) are grouped with Crab Lake for the purpose of quota restrictions. A maximum of five permits per day may be issued for all three entry points COMBINED. Since all three lead to essentially the same chain of lakes, I have selected only the Crab Lake entry point to be included in this trail guide, which offers the easiest and quickest access to this area.

Route #3: The Buck Lake Loop

3 Days, 34 Miles, 10 Lakes, 2 Creeks, 12 Portages
Difficulty: Rugged
Fisher Map: 112 (111 optional)

Introduction: This interesting little route will take you from the south shore access of Burntside through one of the most populated lakes "serving" the BWCA and into one of the least traveled sections of the Boundary Waters — within a time span of less than a day! You'll head north from beautiful big Burntside, across Crab Lake and west through small lakes and tiny streams to Buck Lake. From Buck you'll portage 1½ miles northeast to Cummings Lake, and then travel the length of this pretty lake to Korb Creek. After a side trip to seldom visited Coxey Pond, you'll return to Crab Lake via swampy Korb Creek, and then portage out of this tranquil scene and back into busy Burntside to the boat landing from which you started.

When finished, you will have carried your canoe and packs across portages totalling 1,931 rods (over 6 miles!) Or, if each portage takes TWO trips to get all of your gear across, that means over 18 miles of walking during this weekend outing! That's why this "interesting little route" is called RUGGED. The only people you will see in the interior portion of this route, therefore, are dedicated canoeists: a nice difference from those encountered along the Moose chain of lakes (and others).

Walleye, northern pike, lake trout, bass and bluegill are all found in lakes along this route. Crab and Cummings lakes, in particular, are good spots to try your luck for northerns, bass and bluegill. The experienced angler might find lake trout and small mouth bass in the depths of Burntside Lake. But those who are hungry for walleye should paddle straight for Buck Lake.

Regardless of your fishing luck, you'll surely find the isolated lakes and streams along this route to be a delightful escape for three days full of healthy exercise.

DAY 1: **Burntside Lake,** p. 320 rods, **Crab Lake,** p. 20 rods, **Little Crab Lake, Lunetta Creek, Lunetta Lake,** p. 60 rods, **Lunetta Creek,** p. 100 rods, **Schlamm Lake,** p. 210 rods, **Glenmore Lake.** You will be portaging over 2 miles this day, so don't begin this route unless you are physically ready. Burntside Lake, with well over 100 picturesque islands, could be confusing to even an experienced map reader. Keep constant count of the islands and bays as you weave through them to the Crab Lake portage. None of the portages is difficult, however — just long. Don't be worried if campsites are occupied on Crab Lake. Most weekend traffic either stops here or proceeds on north to Cummings Lake. Nevertheless, remember that campsites are infrequent between Crab and Buck — only one per lake.

DAY 2: **Glenmore Lake,** p. 195 rods, **Western Lake,** p. 80 rods, **Buck Lake,** p. 480 rods, **Cummings Lake.** The westernmost tip of this loop is not shown on Fisher Map 112. So here is what you are missing: After the 195-rod portage from Glenmore Lake, follow the western shore of Western Lake to the northwest corner, where an 80-rod portage will take you to Buck Lake. Paddle to the right (northeast) on this long, narrow lake, to the 480-rod portage that is shown on Map 112. This portage is long, but nothing to worry about. The trail is virtually flat, and there are 16 canoe rests along the way. There are several nice campsites on the east end of Cummings.

DAY 3: **Cummings Lake,** p. 35 rods, **Korb Creek, Korb Lake, Korb Creek,** p. 1-3 rods, **creek, Little Crab Lake,** p. 20 rods, **Crab Lake,** p. 320 rods, **Burntside Lake.** If the water level is high enough and your time permits, you may enjoy a side trip from Korb Creek to Silica Lake and Coxey Pond. These lakes are probably visited more by hikers than canoeists, as the Cummings Lake Trail passes between them. It is about three miles from that point to the North Arm Road (County Road 644).

Route #4: Canadian Border Route

10 Days, 107 Miles, 29 Lakes, 3 Rivers, 6 Creeks, 48 Portages
Difficulty: Challenging
Fisher Maps: 107, 108, 111, 112

Introduction: This route will lead you from the North Arm of Burntside Lake through Crab and Cummings Lakes to the marshy wilderness of the Little Indian Sioux River. Down this meandering little creek, across the Echo Trail and on north to Loon and Slim Lakes, you will then paddle east through the chain of lakes and creeks paralleling Lac La Croix just to the south of this mammoth lake. From the east end of Lac La Croix, you'll continue east across Iron Lake, around impressive Curtain Falls, through the many bays of Crooked Lake, and up the legendary Basswood River. From beautiful lower Basswood Falls you will point your canoe southwest and forge on up the scenic Horse River to Horse Lake and leave the Boundary Waters via Fourtown Lake. Three lakes to the

southwest you'll end this trip at the Nels Lake landing. Unless
you have made prior arrangements to have a vehicle waiting
there, you must walk the final four miles back to the North
Arm access.

This challenging route will require 10 full, strenuous
days for the average group of canoeists, without a layover day.
Strong winds, however, could slow travel considerably on portions of Burntside Lake, the Little Indian Sioux River, Lac La
Croix and Crooked Lake. The Little Indian Sioux River offers
a fine opportunity to view moose, deer, beaver and other forms
of wildlife, as it flows through a region in the BWCA seldom
visited by tourists. Early summer is usually the best season in
which to make this journey, since the Sioux River could be too
dry for navigation later in the summer, especially during a dry
year. Furthermore, your last day (Fourtown to Nels) could be
more walking than paddling when the interconnecting creeks
are too low for loaded canoes.

Although there are numerous portages along the route,
few are longer than 100 rods. Most of the route is well traveled,
with the exception of the Sioux River south of the Echo Trail,
where portage trails may be difficult to see. In addition to the
abundant wildlife and generally good fishing, voyagers may
also find two fine displays of prehistoric Indian pictographs
adorning the sheer granite cliffs of Lac La Croix and the
Basswood River. Splendid waterfalls, treacherous rapids,
beautiful big lakes and quaint little ones all interconnect to
create a fascinating variety of canoeing terrain.

DAY 1: **Burntside Lake,** p. 320 rods, **Crab Lake,** p. 20
rods, **Little Crab Lake, Korb Creek,** p. 1-3 rods, **creek, Korb
Lake, Korb Creek,** p. 35 rods, **Cummings Lake.** Caution:
Burntside Lake can be confusing to even the experienced
guide, so watch carefully for the portage to Crab Lake, in the
third bay west of the "narrows" from the North Arm, along the
north shore of the lake. Several good campsites can be found
near the east end of Cummings Lake. You'll find northern
pike, bass and bluegill inhabiting Crab and Cummings Lake,
trout and bass in Burntside Lake.

DAY 2: **Cummings Lake,** p. 5 rods, **Otter Lake,** p. 120
rods, **Little Indian Sioux River,** p. 28 rods, **river,** p. 20 rods,
river, p. 40 rods, **river,** p. 30 rods, **river,** p. 20 rods, **river,** p. 35
rods, **river,** p. 40 rods, **river.** Campsites are few and far between on this swampy, winding little river, so start looking
while the sun is still high in the sky. In fact, you will find NO
designated USFS campsites unless you portage 376 rods into
Little Trout Lake or 200 rods into Bootleg Lake (both portages

are not only long but hard to find). The nine short portages and considerable meandering make travel deceivingly slow. Between portages it is virtually impossible to know EXACTLY where you are. Use the portages as landmarks, and alert yourself to the GENERAL direction of travel. A decent campsite may be found on the river between the beginnings of the portages into Little Trout and Bootleg lakes.

DAY 3: **Little Indian Sioux River,** p. 20 rods, **river,** p. 120 rods, **river,** p. 8 rods, **river,** p. 120 rods, **river,** p. 60 rods, **river, Upper Pauness Lake.** This will be a long day of paddling, down the gradually widening, deepening and straightening channel of the river. Watch out for traffic as you cross the Echo Trail at the 120-rod portage. From that point on, the number of canoes you see will greatly increase, and motors are permitted. You'll be wise to take the first campsite you see on Upper Pauness Lake.

DAY 4: **Upper Pauness Lake,** p. 8 rods, **Lower Pauness Lake,** p. 160 rods, **Loon Lake, East Loon Bay, Little Loon Lake,** p. 173 rods, **Slim Lake,** p. 52 rods, **Section 3 Pond,** p. 72 rods, **South Lake.** Take time to view the scenic granite gorge through which Devil's Cascade plunges 75 feet from Lower Pauness Lake to Loon Lake. The other half-mile portage this day is uphill, rising 65 feet from Little Loon Lake to Slim Lake. It's steep in some places, and muddy in others, but five canoe rests along the way make portaging a *little* easier. A nice campsite on South Lake is located on a rocky point just to the left of the muddy landing for the portage from Section Three Pond.

DAY 5: **South Lake,** p. 120 rods, **Steep Lake,** p. 45 rods, **Eugene Lake,** p. 50 rods, **Little Bear Track Lake,** p. 30 rods, **Bear Track Lake,** p. 200 rods, **Thumb Lake,** p. 9 rods, **Finger Lake,** p. 90 rods, **Finger Creek, Pocket Lake.** A good, hearty breakfast is a prerequisite this day, as it begins with a steep, uphill portage that climbs 125 feet to Steep Lake. You'll find it to be much tougher than the 200-rod trail between Bear Track and Thumb lakes, which descends 81 feet with a good path and eight canoe rests. You'll find three good campsites on Pocket Lake, and good fishing for northern pike, walleye and bass.

DAY 6: **Pocket Lake,** p. 20 rods, **Pocket Creek,** p. 25 rods, **creek, Lac La Croix.** If you wish, you can probably avoid the 20-rod portage out of Pocket Lake by running, lining or walking the shallow rapids into Pocket Creek. Lac La Croix is the longest and most beautiful of the international lakes bordering the BWCA, dotted with over 200 islands. Pocket

Creek will lead you into the most scenic area of the lake, and numerous good campsites are located near the southeast end. This will be your easiest day of the trip, allowing plenty of time to explore the Indian pictographs (rock paintings) and Warrior Hill (see the Fisher map) found on the Canadian shore. Both monuments are reminders of an ancient civilization that once flourished in this aquatic wilderness. Legend says that Ojibway braves used Warrior Hill to test their strength and courage by racing from the lake's edge to the summit of the precipice. You will truly appreciate this feat after climbing it yourself — and the incredible view from the top will make your effort worthwhile!

DAY 7: **Lac La Croix,** p. 80 rods, **Bottle Lake, Iron Lake,** p. 120 rods, **Crooked Lake.** In addition to the beautiful Curtain Falls between Iron and Crooked lakes, you may also wish to see Rebecca Falls, which slice through two narrow gorges on each side of the island on which the portage into McAree Lake lies. The waterfalls are on both sides of the island, and to view Rebecca, you must first land at the portage and then hike on either side of the island to its north end. Because of the precarious location of this portage, caution must be exercised when approaching it. The swift current flows to either side of the island, and, unless your approach is dead-center to the island, your canoe could be drawn down this dangerous falls. If you are here in July, look for blueberries on the island.

Curtain Falls, on the other hand, will be approached from the bottom. The portage on the US side is not difficult, but steadily uphill. You may put in at any of three locations at the top of the falls: at the very brink of the falls, or about 100 feet farther into Crooked Lake, or yet another 100 feet or so east. The choice is yours, but I prefer the second as the safest one during normal water conditions for a group that may not be strong enough to fight the swift current at the top of the falls. Use your own judgment and be careful!

A beautiful campsite is located on the eastern tip of the large island near the entrance to Saturday Bay. Several good sites are scattered throughout the lake.

DAY 8: **Crooked Lake, Basswood River.** This easy day of paddling will enable you to enjoy the many interesting bays of Crooked Lake and the historic sites along the Basswood River. At least one eagle's nest is located near the east end of Crooked Lake, and it is not unusual to see eagles soaring overhead. Table Rock is a campsite popular among the French-Canadian voyageurs of two hundred years ago. A dis-

play of Indian paintings may be seen along the west shore of
the Basswood River, about a mile downstream from Lower
Basswood Falls. Several fine campsites are located near here.

DAY 9: **Basswood River,** p. 12 rods, **Basswood River,
Horse River,** p. 70 rods, **river,** p. 50 rods, **river, rapids,
river,** p. 50 rods, **river, rapids, river, rapids, Horse Lake,** p.
70 rods, **pond,** p. 10 rods, **Fourtown Lake,** p. 1-3 rods,
Fourtown Lake. After portaging around Basswood Falls before entering the Horse River, you may enjoy paddling beyond
this confluence to scenic Wheelbarrow Falls, about ¾ mile up
the Basswood River. While traveling up the Horse River, you
will encounter at least three short, shallow rapids up which
you will have to pull your canoe. These are located near the
source of the river. Horse and Fourtown Lakes are both BWCA
entry lakes popular among fishermen. In them you'll find
northern pike, walleye and bluegill. Sea planes frequently
bring fishermen to the south end of Fourtown, located outside
the Boundary Waters, and motors are permitted throughout
the lake. You may wish to camp on quieter Horse Lake.

DAY 10: **Fourtown Lake,** p. 10 rods, **Fourtown Creek,**
p. 110 rods, **pond,** p. 30 rods, **Mudro Lake, Mudro Creek,** p.
30 rods, **Picket Lake,** p. 30 rods, **Picket Creek,** p. 185 rods,
Nels Lake. Beware the creeks connecting these four lakes
when the water level is down. They can make life miserable
for the voyager with a heavily loaded canoe. When the water
level is up, on the other hand, you may be able to eliminate the
30-rod portage between Mudro and Picket by paddling or
walking your canoe through this shallow stretch and under
the Cloquet Road (Forest Route 457). Four-wheel-drive vehi-
cles may reach this point from the small town of Winton, two
miles northeast of Ely. Watch your step on that last portage: a
log bridge crosses a creek midway through the carry, and it is
slippery when wet.

Entry Point 6—Slim Lake

Permits: 258
Popularity Rank: 34
Daily Quota: 2

   Location: Slim Lake is 8 miles northwest of Ely, 2 miles west of the Echo Trail and a scant ½ mile north of Burntside Lake. To get there, follow the Echo Trail (County Road 116) 9 miles north and west from County Road 88. Turn left onto County Road 644 (North Arm Road) and follow this winding gravel road southwest for 2 miles to the public access of Burntside Lake on the left.

   Description: On the right side of the road here, you will see a primitive road leading northwest up a gentle slope into the woods. This is the portage trail to Slim Lake. You can either park beside Burntside Lake and portage almost ½ mile to Slim Lake, or drive most of the way up this narrow path to the boundary of the BWCA, within ⅛ mile of Slim Lake. Primitive parking places and turnarounds are scarce along this road, and portions of the road may be under as much as one foot of water. If you are in a four-wheel-drive vehicle, that's no problem; otherwise you probably should park along County Road 644 and hike the entire portage. It is a wide and easy trail, and it ascends quite gently.

   Motors are prohibited through the Slim Lake Entry Point. Although it is close to one of the most popular lakes in the area — Burntside — you will quickly escape into a genuine feeling of wilderness solitude and will experience a high-quality expedition via either of the two routes suggested below.

   Camping is prohibited at the access to Slim Lake. But Fenske Lake Campground, located just 3 miles from here, toward Ely on the Echo Trail, provides a good place to spend the night before your trip.

Route #5: The Big Moose Loop

3 Days, 34 Miles, 12 Lakes, 3 Creeks, 13 Portages
Difficulty: Rugged
Fisher map: 112

   Introduction: This short, rugged journey will take you northwest from the Slim Lake portage, through half a dozen seldom-visited lakes, to the northern edge of this portion of the BWCA at Big Moose Lake. Turning south then, you will cross your longest portage (580 rods) to enter Cummings Lake. Continuing south, you will meander through a series of fascinating little creeks and lakes and exit the Boundary Waters across a mile-long portage into beautiful, big Burntside Lake. Following its northern shoreline, you will soon return to your origin at the Slim Lake portage near the upper end of the North Arm of Burntside.

When finished, you will have spent as much time walking on portage trails as you did paddling on the adjoining scenic lakes. Three portages are in excess of 1½ miles and a fourth is exactly 1 mile. It is largely BECAUSE of these portages, however, that this route is so enticing to the wilderness enthusiast. Only the dedicated canoeist will tackle the route, and it is not unusual to see no other canoeists along that portion of the route contained within the BWCA, where motors are not allowed. You'll feel truly isolated from the rest of the world, even though you will never be more than 5 miles from a road or resort.

Populated Burntside Lake will nearly always be bustling with motorized traffic, and you will witness private cabins, resorts and camps throughout the final 5 miles of your expedition. Were it not for the exceptional beauty of this island-studded lake, the accompanying activity might prove to be a dismal end for an otherwise high-quality wilderness trip.

Fishermen will find northern pike, bass and pan fish along much of the route, and the persistent angler may even pull lake trout from Burntside.

DAY 1: P. 140 rods, **Slim Lake,** p. 77 rods, **Rice Lake,** p. 130 rods, **Hook Lake,** p. 520 rods, **Big Rice Lake.** Portages total 867 rods this day — that's 2,600 rods of walking if you cannot transport all of your gear in one carry! Don't attempt this route unless you are in the *best* of shape! If time permits, I suggest yet another ½ mile of walking (without loads this time). An outstanding panorama can be seen from a high, rocky ridge ¼ mile south of Slim Lake, affectionately named "Old Baldy" by the summer residents of nearby Camp Northland. A blazed trail begins at a Forest Service campsite on the southeast shore of Slim Lake and winds up the thickly wooded hillside. Watch for a spur trail to the left that leads up to the rocky summit. If you miss it and continue walking on the main path, you will eventually find yourself back at County Road 644, near the shore of Burntside's North Arm.

Also if time permits and the season is right, you will find "fields" of blueberries atop the rocky cliffs just north of the Slim Lake end of the portage from Burntside.

DAY 2: **Big Rice Lake,** p. 8 rods, **Big Rice Creek, Lapond Lake,** p. 30 rods, **creek,** p. 150 rods, **Duck Lake,** p. 480 rods, **Big Moose Lake,** p. 580 rods, **Cummings Lake.** If you thought day 1 was unbearable, you might as well stay on Big Rice Lake another night and then backtrack to your origin, because this day is even tougher: 1,248 rods of portages! If you are exhausted by the time you reach Big Moose Lake, rest awhile, but don't give up. The next portage is not as bad as it looks. It begins and ends on a rather hilly note, but follows a rather level ridgetop along most of its course. There are 19 canoe rests along the way.

Several good campsites can be found at the east end of Cummings Lake, including one very large, beautiful site on the east shore, near the Cummings Lake Trail.

DAY 3: **Cummings Lake,** p. 35 rods, **Korb Creek, Korb Lake, Korb Creek,** p. 1-3 rods, **creek, Little Crab Lake,** p. 20 rods, **Crab Lake,** p. 320 rods, **Burntside Lake, North Arm Burntside Lake.** Your last day will be the easiest, by far, so take time to enjoy the pretty little lakes and streams leading toward Burntside. The only major challenge of the day is the 320-rod portage into Burntside Lake, but it will seem like nothing after the ordeal you have already been through. After an initial short climb, the wide, smooth trail slopes gently downhill, and there are 11 canoe rests along the way, should you need a break. The next 2 miles of paddling will surely be the most confusing stretch on this route. Watch carefully for the narrow channel leading northeast into the North Arm.

Route #6: The Meandering Moose Loop

7 Days, 72 Miles, 17 Lakes, 3 Rivers, 2 Creeks, 39 Portages
Difficulty: Rugged
Fisher maps: 107, 112

Introduction: This week-long journey will provide a smorgasbord of scenic terrain, from the tiniest of creeks to the largest of lakes. From the Slim Lake portage, you will paddle north and west through a series of small lakes and streams to Big Moose Lake. Then you will leave the BWCA for a day and head down the meandering Moose River, across the Echo Trail and on north to Nina-Moose Lake. Continuing north, you'll glide down the placid Nina-Moose River to Lake Agnes and eventually to giant Lac La Croix on the Canadian border, where you will stop to view old Indian rock paintings and to climb atop legendary Warrior Hill. From beautiful Lac La

Croix, you will point southeast and paddle into Iron Lake, where you will have an opportunity to view two scenic waterfalls before leaving the Canadian border and traveling southwest to Stuart Lake. Up the Stuart River, you will paddle south, again crossing the Echo Trail, to Big Lake. From there you will retrace your path through the lakes and streams that lead to the Slim Lake portage to the North Arm road.

You will see few other travelers in that portion of the BWCA south of the Echo Trail or along the Stuart River. From the Moose River, north of the Echo Trail, to Lac La Croix, however, where motors are permitted, you will share the waterway with others — but not so many as to spoil it. Lac La Croix itself will probably be the busiest lake on the route, as it receives considerable traffic originating at Crane Lake. Resorts and an Indian reservation are located along its northern shore, and motorboats are not an uncommon sight-sound! Nevertheless, this is one of the most beautiful lakes in all the Boundary Waters, and you will surely enjoy your short visit there. Motors are not permitted on most of the route.

Several LONG portages greet you at the beginning and end of this large loop, the longest being nearly 600 rods. However none in the middle portion are excessive.

If the water level is low, you may find the going rough along the upper part of the Moose River and on the Stuart River, but the lower part of the Moose and all of the Nina-Moose are nearly always navigable.

Anglers will find northern pike and bass along much of the route, as well as lake trout in Lac La Croix and walleye in Lac La Croix and Iron Lake. If you really like fishing, stretch this rugged trip into eight days, instead of seven. You will have much more time to search for the elusive critters.

DAY 1: p. 140 rods, **Slim Lake,** p. 77 rods, **Rice Lake,** p. 130 rods, **Hook Lake,** p. 520 rods, **Big Rice Lake.** (See comments for Day 1, Route #5.)

DAY 2: **Big Rice Lake,** p. 8 rods, **creek, Lapond Lake,** p. 30 rods, **creek,** p. 150 rods, **Duck Lake,** p. 480 rods, **Big Moose Lake.** Although one LONG portage awaits you this day, you are not expected to go far. Big Moose Lake will offer you several attractive campsites. But there are no Forest Service sites designated along the Moose River. Make camp early, and plan to break camp early the following morning.

DAY 3: **Big Moose Lake,** p. 60 rods, **Moose River,** p. 160 rods, **river,** p. 17 rods, **river,** p. 40 rods, **river,** p. 40 rods, **river,** p. 77 rods, **river,** p. 160 rods, **river,** p. 20 rods, **river,** p. 25 rods, **river, Nina-Moose Lake.** Travel is deceivingly slow on this meandering little stream. Without an early start, you may not make it to Nina-Moose Lake before dusk. You will cross under a spur of the Echo Trail and the Echo Trail itself, and be outside the BWCA most of the day. Canoe traffic is bound to increase beyond the Moose River parking lot north of the Echo Trail, which serves the most popular entry point along the Echo Trail. Find a campsite early on Nina-Moose Lake and try your luck at catching the northern pike, walleye and bass that inhabit this shallow lake. Along the western shoreline you will see evidence of the 1971 fire that ravaged nearly 25 square miles of woodland between here and the Little Indian Sioux River.

DAY 4: **Nina-Moose Lake, Nina-Moose River,** p. 70 rods, **river,** p. 96 rods, **river, Lake Agnes,** p. 24 rods, **Boulder Bay,** p. 65 rods, **Lac La Croix.** This will be the easiest day of your trip, but there is plenty to see and do, so you won't get bored! You'll find a fascinating display of ancient Indian pictographs adorning the sheer granite cliffs along the Canadian shore, about 2 miles north of Boulder Bay. Less than a mile south, you will find "Warrior Hill," where legends tell of Indian braves racing to the summit of this awesome cliff to prove their strength and courage. A climb to the top will reveal a spectacular panorama, and you will develop an instant respect for the Indians who could RUN to the top.

DAY 5: **Lac La Croix,** p. 80 rods, **Bottle Lake, Iron Lake,** p. 72 rods, **Dark Lake,** p. 67 rods, **Rush Lake,** p. 60 rods, **Fox Lake,** p. 320 rods, **Stuart Lake.** If time permits, you will surely enjoy making a short side trip to view two of the more spectacular waterfalls in this part of the BWCA. Rebecca Falls are located at the northern outlet of Iron Lake, where they plunge 23 feet across jagged rocks into McAree Lake. Use caution as you approach these falls. The swift current above them flows to either side of a narrow island, upon which is located the portage to the bottom. You must land on the island at the top of the split falls and hike along its perimeter to view the spectacle. If the season is right, you will find literally thousands of blueberries decorating the island. Curtain Falls, on the other hand, is quite safe, since you will be approaching it from the bottom. It drops a total of 29 gorgeous feet on its way from Crooked Lake to Iron Lake. An outstanding lunch spot is found about midway up the torrent on an outcropping of rock below the main drop of water.

Beware the series of hilly portages between Iron and Stuart lakes. The first three are short, but steep; the last is a mile long!

DAY 6: **Stuart Lake,** p. 80 rods, **Stuart River,** p. 8 rods, **river,** p. 14 rods, **river,** p. 74 rods, **river,** p. 30 rods, **river,** p. 95 rods, **river,** p. 600 rods, **Big Lake.** Your last portage of the day is the longest one of the trip, and mostly uphill. When you see the Echo Trail, continue on across the road (with caution) and Big Lake won't be far away.

DAY 7: **Big Lake,** p. 150 rods, **Lapond Lake, creek,** p. 8 rods, **Big Rice Lake,** p. 520 rods, **Hook Lake,** p. 130 rods, **Rice Lake,** p. 77 rods, **Slim Lake,** p. 140 rods. Beyond the first portage of this day, the route should all look familiar to you. (See Day 1 of Route #5 for comments.)

Entry Point 7—Big Lake

Permits: 34
Popularity Rank: 60
Daily Quota: 1

Location: Big Lake is located 12 miles northwest of Ely, just south of the Echo Trail. To get there, follow the Echo Trail for 18 miles from County Road 88, 10 miles past the point at which it turns to gravel. Drive with caution on this narrow, winding road, particularly for the last 8 miles. Traffic is not heavy, but there is always some, because two resorts are located on Big Lake.

Description: The public campground at Fenske Lake, 10 miles closer to Ely on the Echo Trail, provides a good place to spend the night before your canoe trip.

Very few people use Big Lake to enter the Boundary Waters, and most of the BWCA south of the Echo Trail is very lightly used. You will find a high quality wilderness experience using either of the routes mentioned below. Motors are prohibited through this entry point.

Route #7: The Slim-Crab Loop

3 Days, 38 Miles, 13 Lakes, 3 Creeks, 13 Portages
Difficulty: Rugged
Fisher map: 112

Introduction: This difficult route will take you south from Big Lake through a series of small lakes and streams to big Burntside Lake, located south of the BWCA. You will follow the north shore of Burntside southwest to the long portage into Crab Lake. Through another series of small scenic lakes and streams, you will paddle northward to the longest portage of the trip, into Big Moose Lake. From Big Moose you will take another long walk, to Duck Lake, and continue to work your way east back to your origin on Big Lake. When finished, you will think that you walked as much as you paddled — and perhaps you did! Three portages are in excess of 1½ miles! Because of these long treks, only the dedicated canoeist will tackle the route, and it is not unusual to see no other canoeists along that portion of the loop contained within the BWCA, where motors are not allowed. You feel worlds away from your nearest neighbor, when, in fact, you will never be more than 5 miles from a road or resort.

Populated Lake Burntside will nearly always be bustling

with motorized traffic, however, and you will witness private cabins, resorts and camps throughout your stretch on this beautiful, island-studded lake.

Fishermen will find northern pike, bass and pan fish along much of the route, and the persistent angler may even pull lake trout from the depths of Burntside Lake.

DAY 1: **Big Lake,** p. 150 rods, **Lapond Lake, Big Rice Creek,** p. 8 rods, **Big Rice Lake,** p. 520 rods, **Hook Lake,** p. 130 rods, **Rice Lake,** p. 77 rods, **Slim Lake.** If you are not in the best of shape, be prepared for mighty sore muscles at day's end. But if you still have some energy, you'll find two treats at the south end of Slim Lake. A blazed trail begins at a Forest Service campsite on the southeast shore of Slim Lake that winds up the thickly wooded hillside to a trail that spurs off to the left and leads to a high, rocky ridge ¼ mile south of Slim Lake. Affectionately named "Old Baldy" by the summer residents of nearby Camp Northland, this summit affords an outstanding panorama of the surrounding woodlands. Watch for the spur trail. If you continue on the main trail, you will eventually find yourself on County Road 644, a mile to the south.

If you have arrived here during the right season, you will find blueberries atop Old Baldy, as well as along the rocky cliffs just north of the Slim Lake end of the portage from Burntside.

DAY 2: **Slim Lake,** p. 140 rods, **North Arm Burntside Lake, Burntside Lake,** p. 320 rods, **Crab Lake,** p. 20 rods, **Little Crab Lake, Korb Creek,** p. 1-3 rods, **creek, Korb Lake, Korb Creek,** p. 35 rods, **Cummings Lake.** You will find the mile-long portage into Crab Lake to be mostly uphill, but it slopes gently and follows a good path, and 11 canoe rests are situated evenly along the trail. A very nice campsite for a large group is located on the west shore of Cummings Lake, near the Cummings Lake Trail.

DAY 3: **Cummings Lake,** p. 580 rods, **Big Moose Lake,** p. 480 rods, **Duck Lake,** p. 150 rods, **Portage River, Big Lake.** Your three big portages total 1,210 rods; and if you can't carry all of your gear in one trip, that means over *11 miles* of walking. Your friends back home will never believe it! Fortunately, your longest portage of the route (between Cummings and Big Moose) is mostly level, with only a few small hills at each end. Nineteen canoe rests are useful in determining how far you have walked, even if you don't need them for rests.

Route #8: The Grassy-Beartrap Route

6 Days, 54 Miles, 31 Lakes, 4 Rivers, 2 Creeks, 42 Portages
Difficulty: Rugged
Fisher maps: 107, 108, 112

Introduction: This large, fascinating loop will take you south from Big Lake to Burntside Lake, and then northeast through many picturesque small lakes and streams to two popular fishing lakes, Horse and Fourtown. From Fourtown Lake you will angle off to the northwest and paddle through several small lakes to the Beartrap River. About halfway down the Beartrap River you will branch off on Sterling Creek and follow it west to Sterling Lake and eventually on to Stuart Lake. Then you will turn south and paddle up the Stuart River to your origin at Big Lake.

Much of your trip will be spent on small, winding streams and scenic little lakes, most of which are off limits to motorists. Nearly two full days of travel, however, will be outside of the Boundary Waters, as you cross through the Echo Trail region between the Slim Lake and Horse Lake entry points. This region, along with Fourtown Lake, is the only portion of the route where motors are permitted. Most of the loop receives light to moderate use, the immediate vicinity of Burntside Lake being the only exception.

Water level is a critical factor for the navigation of this route. Passage could be difficult or impossible in most of the rivers and creeks during periods of extremely low water.

Fishermen will find walleye, northern pike and pan fish along much of the route. Fourtown and Horse lakes, in particular, are popular among anglers, as evidenced by the frequent landings of float planes on the south end of Fourtown, which is outside the BWCA.

DAY 1: **Big Lake,** p. 150 rods, **Lapond Lake, Big Rice Creek,** p. 8 rods, **Big Rice Lake,** p. 520 rods, **Hook Lake,** p. 130 rods, **Rice Lake,** p. 77 rods, **Slim Lake.** (See comments for Day 1 of Route #7.)

DAY 2: **Slim Lake,** p. 140 rods, **North Arm Burntside Lake,** p. 250 rods, **West Twin Lake, East Twin Lake,** p. 14 rods, **Everett Lake,** p. 120 rods, **Fenske Lake,** p. 10 rods, **Little Sletten Lake,** p. 70 rods, **Sletten Lake,** p. 120 rods, **Tee Lake,** p. 48 rods, **Grassy Lake.** None of the portages is difficult, but their frequency slows travel considerably. The only serious uphill challenge is the 70-rod path between Little Sletten and Sletten lakes. You will see several cabins and resorts from Burntside to Fenske Lake, but the small lakes east of the Echo Trail are quite uncivilized.

DAY 3: **Grassy Lake, beaver pond,** p. 24 rods, **Grassy River, Range River,** p. 1 rod, **river,** p. 30 rods, **river,** p. 10 rods, **river, Range Lake,** p. 340 rods, **Tin Can Lake.** If the water level is low, you may find a short portage between Grassy Lake and the beaver pond. The 2-rod portage on the Range River is merely a liftover where the Cloquet Road crosses the river. (See the sketch of the Range River area below.) Beaver dams are not uncommon on portions of the Range River. If you wish, you may break your 340-rod carry between Range and Tin Can lakes into two 160-rod portages, with a few rods of paddling on Sandpit Lake in between them. The trails here may be somewhat confusing, with the map offering little for clarification. You will be following an old railroad bed part of the way.

DAY 4: **Tin Can Lake,** p. 90 rods, **Horse Lake,** p. 70 rods, **pond,** p. 10 rods, **Fourtown Lake,** p. 1-3 rods, **Fourtown Lake,** p. 35 rods, **Boot Lake,** p. 15 rods, **Fairy Lake,** p. 50 rods, **Gun Lake,** p. 30 rods, **Gull Lake,** p. 35 rods, **Mudhole Lake,** p. 55 rods, **Thunder Lake.** Unlike its neighbors on either side, Fourtown Lake is a designated motor route. Beyond it, however, the lakes are "paddle only," and rather lightly traveled. You should encounter no difficulty on the portages this day.

DAY 5: **Thunder Lake,** p. 9 rods, **Beartrap Lake,** p. 200 rods, **Beartrap River,** p. 160 rods, **river, Sunday Lake,** p. 8 rods, **river, Sterling Creek, Sterling Lake,** p. 148 rods, **Bibon Lake,** p. 10 rods, **Nibin Lake,** p. 180 rods, **Stuart Lake.** Although two big portages present themselves early this day, both are predominantly downhill. In fact you will descend nearly 100 feet in all between Beartrap and Sunday lakes.

DAY 6: **Stuart Lake,** p. 80 rods, **Stuart River,** p. 8 rods, **river,** p. 14 rods, **river,** p. 74 rods, **river,** p. 30 rods, **river,** p. 95 rods, **river,** p. 600 rods, **Big Lake.** No Forest Service campsites are located along the Stuart River. Should you get a late start this morning or find it necessary to make an early camp, there is a campsite on White Feather Lake, accessible through a short stream that connects to the Stuart River just south of the 74-rod portage.

The Range River

Grassy Lake

Grassy River

p. 24r

Range River

p. 30r

p. 1r

p. 10r

Forest Route 457
"Cloquet Road"

Range Lake

p. 160r

Sandpit Lake

p. 40r

p. 20r

Tin Can Lake

Jackfish Bay of Basswood Lake

Range Lake

p. 160r

Sandpit Lake

p. 160r

p. 130r

p. 20r

p. 20r

p. 40r

Tin Can Lake

Jackfish Bay

Entry Point 8—Big Moose Lake

Permits: 32
Popularity Rank: 62
Daily Quota: 2

Location: Big Moose Lake is located about 13 miles northwest of Ely, and 3 miles south of the Echo Trail. To drive there, follow the Echo Trail for 21 miles from County Road 88. Turn left onto Forest Route 464 and follow it for 3½ miles to the Moose River, which leads to Big Moose Lake.

Description: The river leading to Big Moose Lake meanders considerably, and during dry periods it could be too shallow for navigation. Because of its difficulty of access, and the long portage (580 rods) at its south end, Big Moose Lake is used by VERY few canoeists entering the Boundary Waters. Consequently, a high-quality wilderness experience can be found on either of the excellent routes described below.

The nearest Forest Service campground is at Lake Jeanette, 12 miles farther west on the Echo Trail from its junction with Forest Route 464. Or perhaps you would like to stop at the Fenske Lake campground, 8 miles from County Road 88 on the Echo Trail.

The northern third of Big Moose Lake is outside of the BWCA, but motorboats are not allowed into the Boundary Waters at this point of entry. This wide-open lake is a beautiful sight after your winding approach through the upper reaches of the tiny Moose River.

Route #9: The Crab-Slim Loop

4 Days, 37 Miles, 12 Lakes, 1 River, 3 Creeks, 17 Portages
Difficulty: Rugged
Fisher map: 112

Introduction: This exhausting route is recommended for only the heartiest of voyagers. From Big Moose Lake you will portage nearly 2 miles south to Cummings Lake. Continuing south through a series of small, picturesque lakes and streams, you will then portage another mile, out of the BWCA into beautiful Burntside Lake. Weaving your way through the confusing maze of islands and into the North Arm of this populated lake, you will then portage back into the Boundary Waters via the Slim Lake entry point. You will continue paddling northwest through the small lakes and tiny streams and carrying your gear across the LONG portages that lead back to Big Moose, from which you will retrace your path back down the Moose River to the landing at Forest Route 464.

When finished, you will have spent as much time walking on portage trails as you did paddling on the adjoining scenic lakes. Three portages are longer than 1½ miles and a fourth is exactly 1 mile. It is largely BECAUSE of these portages, however, that this route is so enticing to the wilderness enthusiast. Only the truly dedicated canoeist will tackle the route, and it is not unusual to see no other canoeists along that portion of the route contained within the BWCA, where motors are not allowed. You will feel truly isolated from the rest of the world, even though you will never be more than 5 miles from a resort or road.

Nevertheless, Burntside Lake will nearly always be bustling with motorized traffic, and you will pass private cabins, resorts and camps throughout this portion of your trip. Were it not for the exceptional beauty of this island-studded lake, the accompanying activity might prove to be a dismal part of an otherwise high-quality wilderness trip.

Fishermen will find northern pike, bass and pan fish along much of the route, and the persistent angler may even pull lake trout from Burntside Lake.

DAY 1: **Moose River,** p. 160 rods, **river,** p. 60 rods, **Big Moose Lake,** p. 580 rods, **Cummings Lake.** Don't let the 580-rod portage scare you; it's long, but not too difficult. Although the beginning is uphill and overgrown in places, the path soon levels off, and then follows a ridgetop along most of its course. Nineteen canoe rests make life a little easier, too. Several good campsites are at the east end of Cummings Lake, including a very large, nice site on the east shore, near the Cummings Lake Trail.

DAY 2: **Cummings Lake,** p. 35 rods, **Korb Creek, Korb Lake, Korb Creek,** p. 1-3 rods, **creek, Little Crab Lake,** p. 20 rods, **Crab Lake,** p. 320 rods, **Burntside Lake,** p. 140 rods, **Slim Lake.** This will be the easiest day of the trip, by far. The only major challenge is the one-mile portage into Burntside Lake. After an initial short climb, the wide, smooth trail slopes gently downhill, and there are 11 canoe rests along the way. The next 2 miles of paddling will be the most confusing stretch of this route, so watch carefully for the narrow channel leading northeast into the North Arm of Burntside.

If time permits at the day's end, you may wish to visit "Old Baldy," a high, rocky ridge ¼ mile south of Slim Lake. (See comments for Day 1, Route #7.)

DAY 3: **Slim Lake,** p. 77 rods, **Rice Lake,** p. 130 rods,

Hook Lake, p. 520 rods, **Big Rice Lake,** p. 8 rods, **creek, Lapond Lake.** If the season is right, you may enjoy picking blueberries along the east shore of Slim Lake, for there are "fields" of blueberries atop the rocky cliffs just north of the Slim Lake end of the portage from Burntside Lake.

DAY 4: **Lapond Lake,** p. 30 rods, **creek,** p. 150 rods, **Duck Lake,** p. 480 rods, **Big Moose Lake,** p. 60 rods, **Moose River,** p. 160 rods, **river.** If an emergency arises or if for any other reason you decide to terminate your expedition early, portage 150 rods from the north shore of Lapond Lake into Big Lake. Two resorts are located on the north shore, and there you will find easy access to the Echo Trail.

Route #10: The Sioux-Border Loop

8 Days, 82 Miles, 20 Lakes, 3 Rivers, 2 Creeks, 42 Portages
Difficulty: Rugged
Fisher maps: 107, 111, 112

Introduction: This elongated loop will first take you south from Big Moose Lake across the long 580-rod portage to Cummings Lake. From there you will turn west and paddle into the headwaters of the Little Indian Sioux River, which will continue meandering to the west for several miles before bending northward, crossing the Echo Trail and eventually entering the Pauness lakes. You will portage around scenic Devil's Cascade and proceed into Loon Lake and then northeast to South Lake. Then you will point eastward and navigate the small lakes and streams that lead to the southeast portion of beautiful Lac La Croix, where you will have an opportunity to see Indian pictographs and climb legendary Warrior Hill. After going southwest to Lake Agnes, you will paddle up the Nina-Moose River to Nina-Moose Lake. Continuing south, you will re-enter the Moose River and follow its course across the Echo Trail to Forest Route 464 and the point where this journey originated.

The whole route will require eight full, strenuous days for the average group of canoeists, plus any layover days. If strong winds prevail, you may find the going slowed considerably on portions of the Indian Sioux River. Early summer is usually the best time to make this trip, since the Sioux and Moose rivers could be too shallow later in the summer, especially during a dry year.

Most of the route south of the Echo Trail is not heavily used, and the portage trails may sometimes be hard to see. Along the Indian Sioux River, wildlife is plentiful, including moose, deer and beaver. North of the Echo Trail, however, where both the Indian Sioux and Moose rivers are designated motor routes, you will see many more canoes. But even there, use is moderate, except on the ever-popular Lac La Croix. In general, if you like to paddle on slow, meandering little streams, and you don't mind frequent — and occasionally long — portaging, you will find this route delightful.

DAY 1: **Moose River,** p. 160 rods, **river,** p. 60 rods, **Big Moose Lake,** p. 580 rods, **Cummings Lake.** (See comments for Day 1, Route #9.)

DAY 2: **Cummings Lake,** p. 5 rods, **Otter Lake,** p. 120 rods, **Little Indian Sioux River,** p. 28 rods, **river,** p. 20 rods, **river,** p. 40 rods, **river,** p. 30 rods, **river,** p. 20 rods, **river,** p. 35 rods, **river,** p. 40 rods, **river.** Campsites are few and far between on this swampy, winding little river, so start looking while the sun is still high in the sky. In fact, you will find NO designated Forest Service campsites unless you portage 376 rods into Little Trout Lake or 200 rods into Bootleg Lake (both portages are not only long but also hard to find). The nine short portages and considerable meandering make travel deceivingly slow. Between portages it is virtually impossible to know EXACTLY where you are. Use the portages as landmarks, and alert yourself to the GENERAL direction of travel. A decent campsite may be found on the river between the portages into Little Trout and Bootleg lakes.

DAY 3: **Little Indian Sioux River,** p. 20 rods, **river,** p. 120 rods, **river,** p. 8 rods, **river,** p. 120 rods, **river,** p. 60 rods, **river, Upper Pauness Lake.** This will be a long day of paddling down the gradually widening, deepening and straightening channel of the river. Watch out for traffic as you cross the Echo Trail at the 120-rod portage. From that point on, where motors are permitted, the number of canoes you see will greatly increase. You will be wise to grab the first campsite you see on Upper Pauness Lake.

DAY 4: **Upper Pauness Lake,** p. 8 rods, **Lower Pauness Lake,** p. 160 rods, **Loon Lake, East Loon Bay, Little Loon Lake,** p. 173 rods, **Slim Lake,** p. 52 rods, **Section Three Pond,** p. 72 rods, **South Lake.** Take time to view the scenic granite gorge through which Devil's Cascade plunges 75 feet from Lower Pauness Lake to Loon Lake. The other half-mile portage this day is uphill, rising 65 feet from Little Loon Lake to Slim Lake. It is steep in some places and muddy in others, but five canoe rests along the way make portaging a LITTLE easier. A nice campsite on South Lake is located on a rocky point just left of the muddy landing for the portage from Section Three Pond.

DAY 5: **South Lake,** p. 120 rods, **Steep Lake,** p. 45 rods, **Eugene Lake,** p. 50 rods, **Little Bear Track Lake,** p. 30 rods, **Bear Track Lake,** p. 200 rods, **Thumb Lake,** p. 9 rods, **Finger Lake,** p. 90 rods, **Finger Creek, Pocket Lake.** This day starts out with a steep portage that climbs 125 feet to Steep Lake. You will find it much tougher than the 200-rod trail between Bear Track and Thumb lakes, which descends 81 feet on a good path with eight canoe rests. There are three good campsites on Pocket Lake, and good fishing for northern pike, walleye and bass.

DAY 6: **Pocket Lake,** p. 20 rods, **Pocket Creek,** p. 25 rods, **creek, Lac La Croix.** If you wish, you can probably avoid the 20-rod portage out of Pocket Lake by running, lining, or walking the shallow rapids into Pocket Creek. Lac La Croix, dotted with over 200 islands, is the longest and one of the most beautiful of the international lakes bordering the BWCA. This will be the easiest day of your trip, allowing plenty of time for you to explore the Indian rock paintings and Warrior Hill, found on the Canadian shoreline. Both monuments are reminders of an ancient civilization that once flourished in this aquatic wilderness. Legend says that Ojibway braves used Warrior Hill to test their strength and courage by racing from lake's edge to the summit. You will appreciate this feat only after climbing it yourself, and the incredible view from the top will make your effort worthwhile.

DAY 7: **Lac La Croix,** p. 65 rods, **Boulder Bay,** p. 24 rods, **Lake Agnes, Nina-Moose River,** p. 96 rods, **river,** p. 70 rods, **river, Nina-Moose Lake.** This day takes you through the most heavily traveled portion of the entire route. Be psychologically prepared for company.

DAY 8: **Nina-Moose Lake, Moose River,** p. 25 rods, **river,** p. 20 rods, **river,** p. 160 rods, **river,** p. 77 rods, **river,** p. 40 rods, **river,** p. 40 rods, **river,** p. 17 rods, **river.** The Moose River is another narrow, winding little stream through marshy terrain. Almost choked with vegetation during prime summer months, your route is frequently visible scarcely more than a few yards in front of the canoe. Travel is slow, as you are paddling against the current and meandering considerably. The 160-rod portage will take you into the parking lot serving the Moose River entry point. Bear to the right (west) and you will find the river again just past the parking area.

Entry Point 9—Little Indian Sioux River - South

Permits: 34
Popularity Rank: 60
Daily Quota: 1

Location: The Little Indian Sioux River begins its winding course about 15 miles northwest of Ely. It flows west for about 6 miles and then turns north and eventually flows into Loon Lake on the Canadian border. All the river except that part in the immediate vicinity of the Echo Trail is contained within the BWCA. The upper part of the river (south of the Echo Trail) is accessible via the Sioux River-South entry point (#9), while the lower, northern part is served by the Sioux River-North entry point (#14). To get to the accesses, follow the Echo Trail for 28 miles from County Road 88. The South access is below the bridge on the left side of the road.

Description: You may wish to spend the night before your trip at a public campground 4 miles west on the Echo Trail, at Jeanette Lake. This will enable an early start the following morning — and you will need it!

This entry point leads into one of the least traveled, most pristine areas within the Boundary Waters, offering as much solitude and bountiful wildlife as you would ever hope to encounter. The Little Indian Sioux River provides a good opportunity to view moose, deer, beaver and other wildlife. It is most suitable early in the summer, when the water level is usually up. During dry spells, the river could be too shallow for navigation with loaded canoes. Regardless of the date, you will surely see few if any other canoes on this slow and weedy stream.

Route #11: Trout-Cummings Lakes Loop

5 Days, 55 Miles, 12 Lakes, 1 River, 4 Creeks, 26 Portages
Difficulty: Rugged
Fisher maps: 111, 112

Introduction: This high-quality wilderness expedition will take you up the Little Indian Sioux River and into Little Trout Lake. Continuing south, you will paddle into giant Trout Lake, and then turn east and follow a chain of interesting little lakes and streams to Little Crab Lake. From there, you will paddle north into Korb and Cummings lakes, before turning west and re-entering the Little Indian Sioux River, which leads you back north to your origin on the Echo Trail.

You will find fishing good in many of the lakes along this route. Try for northern pike or bass in Cummings, Otter, Little Trout and Trout lakes. Pull a walleye out of Chad, Buck, Little Trout or Trout Lake. Or, if the thought of lake trout sounds especially good, take time to fish the lower depths of Trout Lake.

You will feel truly isolated throughout most of this route. But during your brief swing through the northeastern corner of Trout Lake, you may see dozens of motor boats with anglers testing their luck for lake trout. The motor route through Trout Lake is one of the busiest in the BWCA. But, rest assured, the commotion won't extend beyond Little Trout Lake, or Pine Creek. The rest of this route will be shared with few, if any, other canoeists.

DAY 1: **Little Indian Sioux River,** p. 8. rods, **river,** p. 120 rods, **river,** p. 20 rods, **river,** p. 376 rods, **Little Trout Lake.** Get an early start this day, as you will surely find the going to be slow on this winding little stream. And if a strong south wind prevails, you will have that to contend with too. There are no Forest Service campsites on the river, so it is important that you reach Little Trout Lake in time to find a site. Watch carefully for the 376-rod portage, as it may pass by unnoticed. If you come to a 40-rod portage on the river, you will know you have just passed the long one, which is not well-traveled and may be muddy, but has no major inclines.

DAY 2: **Little Trout Lake, Little Trout Creek, Trout Lake, Pine Creek,** p. 40 rods, **creek,** p. 260 rods, **Chad Lake,** p. 250 rods, **Buck Lake,** p. 80 rods, **Western Lake.** Be prepared for the first long portage. It steeply climbs nearly 100 feet above Pine Creek before descending gradually to Chad Lake. On the 250-rod portage between Buck and Chad lakes over a 50-foot hill, notice how the interconnecting stream changes direction midway across the portage.

DAY 3: **Western Lake,** p. 195 rods, **Clenmore Lake,** p. 210 rods, **Schlamm Lake,** p. 100 rods, **Lunetta Creek,** p. 60 rods, **Lunetta Lake, Lunetta Creek, Little Crab Lake, Korb Creek,** p. 1-3 rods, **creek, Korb Lake, Korb Creek,** p. 35 rods, **Cummings Lake.** None of the portages this day is difficult, although the 210-rod trail between Glenmore and Schlamm lakes climbs 84 feet over a hill. On the 100-rod portage from Schlamm Lake, the path veers off to the right on a gravel road for about 8 rods up a small creek that flows into it. Occasional beaver dams may obstruct your passage on the creek leading into Little Crab Lake. These will require nothing more than a quick liftover, however. The short rapids on the creek leading into Korb Lake may be tempting, but beware the rocky ledge over which it passes. You will find several good campsites at the east end of Cummings Lake, including a large, nice site on the east shore near the Cummings Lake Trail.

DAY 4: **Cummings Lake,** p. 5 rods, **Otter Lake,** p. 120 rods, **Little Indian Sioux River,** p. 28 rods, **river,** p. 20 rods, **river,** p. 40 rods, **river,** p. 30 rods, **river,** p. 20 rods, **river,** p.35 rods, **river,** p. 40 rods, **river.** There are no Forest Service campsites along the Little Indian Sioux River, so unless you portage back into Little Trout Lake or tackle the 200-rod portage into Bootleg Lake, you had better start looking for suitable sites while the sun is still high in the sky. The nine short portages and the river's considerable meandering make travel deceivingly slow. Between portages it is virtually impossible to know exactly where you are. Use the portages as landmarks, and alert yourself to the GENERAL direction of travel. A decent campsite may be found on the river between the portages to Little Trout and Bootleg lakes.

DAY 5: **Little Indian Sioux River,** p. 20 rods, **river,** p. 120 rods, **river,** p. 8 rods, **river.** All of your last day will be spent backtracking the part of the river that you paddled on the first day. If you prefer a change of scenery, portage 200 rods into Bootleg Lake and then follow the Little Pony River north to its junction with the Indian Sioux just above the 120-rod portage.

Route #12: The Crooked-Oyster Route

10 Days, 110 Miles, 29 Lakes, 6 Rivers, 1 Creek, 49 Portages
Difficulty: Rugged
Fisher maps: 107, 108, 111, 112

Introduction: This long loop will first take you south and east up the Indian Sioux River to Cummings Lake. Continuing south, you'll paddle through several small lakes and creeks and leave the BWCA via the Crab Lake portage into Burntside Lake. Through the Dead River you will then pass into a plethora of tiny lakes and adjoining portages leading northeast to the Range River, which continues northeast back into the BWCA and on to Jackfish Bay, the westernmost bay of enormous Basswood Lake. From the northwest corner of mighty Basswood, you will follow the Canadian border down the beautiful Basswood River, past three lovely waterfalls and a display of Indian rock paintings, to Crooked Lake, a challenge for any map reader. Continuing west along the border you will pass yet another scenic waterfall on your way to island-studded Lac La Croix. From here you will leave the land of the Maple Leaf and turn southwest through a chain of less-traveled lakes and streams connected by rugged portages, to the Pauness lakes. Here you will turn south and again paddle up the lazy Little Indian Sioux River to your origin at the Echo Trail.

When finished, you will have paddled through one of the most varied and beautiful routes in all the BWCA — tiny lakes and mammoth ones, narrow streams and meandering rivers, gorgeous waterfalls, lovely rapids and menacing beaver dams all join together for an unforgettable journey into the domain once inhabited by the Chippewa and woodland Sioux Indians. Motors are prohibited on most of the route, and at times you will see no other canoeists. But during your brief interlude outside of the Boundary Waters, you will surely encounter numerous motorboats, cabins and resorts from Burntside Lake to Fenske Lake, where you must also cross the Echo Trail. But you should not find this part of the route dull, for Burntside is dotted with countless islands that enhance the beauty of this popular lake and the tiny lakes just east of the Echo Trail are as attractive as any found within the designated wilderness area.

Most of the route is easily navigable during any season. The Indian Sioux and Range rivers, however, may offer difficult passage when the water level is low. Normally, the best time for such a trip is in early summer or after the autumn rains. Parts of the route may be impassable during the dry month of August. Wind may also be a potential hazard on this route, particularly on Jackfish Bay. Basswood Lake is notorious for its high, dangerous waves on windy days.

Fishing is generally good throughout most of the route for walleye and northern pike. You will also have an opportunity to fish for lake trout in Basswood, Burntside and Oyster lakes and Lac La Croix. One of the largest northern pike I have seen caught was pulled out of the Basswood River, a ways below Lower Basswood Falls.

DAY 1: **Little Indian Sioux River,** p. 8 rods, **river,** p. 120 rods, **river, Little Pony River,** p. 60 rods, **river,** p. 60 rods, **Bootleg Lake,** (See comments for Days 4 and 5, Route #11.)

DAY 2: **Bootleg Lake,** p. 200 rods, **Little Indian Sioux River,** p. 40 rods, **river,** p. 35 rods, **river,** p. 20 rods, **river,** p.

30 rods, **river,** p. 40 rods, **river,** p. 20 rods, **river,** p. 28 rods, **river,** p. 120 rods, **Otter Lake,** p. 5 rods, **Cummings Lake.** (See comments for Days 4 and 5, Route #11.) Several nice campsites are found near the east end of Cummings Lake.

DAY 3: **Cummings Lake,** p. 35 rods, **Korb Creek, Korb Lake, Korb Creek,** p. 1-3 rods, **creek, Little Crab Lake,** p. 20 rods, **Crab Lake,** p. 320 rods, **Burntside Lake, Dead River, East Twin Lake.** If you are tired of paddling on small streams by now, bypass lower Korb Creek and nearly all of Korb Lake by portaging 70 rods from the South bay of Cummings Lake into the west end of Korb Lake. Your only real challenge of this day is the 1-mile portage into Burntside Lake. It starts out climbing a small hill, but most of the trail is downhill, with a good, wide path and 11 canoe rests along the way. With well over 100 islands, Burntside Lake may be confusing to even the experienced map reader. Watch carefully for the bay from which the Dead River flows toward Twin Lakes. You will find three small, relatively new Forest Service campsites bordering East Twin Lake, but the largest and best site is an undeveloped one on the north side of the portage between East Twin Lake and Everett Lake.

DAY 4: **East Twin Lake,** p. 14 rods, **Everett Lake,** p. 120 rods, **Fenske Lake,** p. 10 rods, **Little Sletten Lake,** p. 70 rods, **Sletten Lake,** p. 120 rods, **Tee Lake,** p. 48 rods, **Grassy Lake, Beaver Pond,** p. 24 rods, **Grassy River, Range River,** p. 1 rod, **river,** p. 30 rods, **river,** p. 10 rods, **river, Range Lake,** p. 130 rods, **Range River,** p. 20 rods, **river, Jackfish Bay.** Of the many portages you will walk today, the only exhausting one is the 70-rod trail which surmounts a steep hill between Little Sletten and Sletten lakes. There may be beaver dams between Grassy Lake and the pond thereafter, as well as on the upper portion of the Grassy River and the lower stretches of the slow, winding, marshy Range River, near Range Lake. When portaging out of Range Lake, bear to the right as the trail divides. This will lead you directly to the Range River, on your way to Jackfish Bay. (otherwise you will portage 160 rods to Sandpit Lake and then must come back down the Range River and cross another 40-rod trail to get to the same location reached by the 130-rod portage.)

DAY 5: **Jackfish Bay, Basswood Lake,** p. 330 rods, **Basswood River,** p. 32 rods, **river,** p. 18 rods, **river,** p. 12 rods, **river.** Three portages this day circumnagivate three scenic waterfalls: Basswood Falls, Wheelbarrow Falls and Lower Basswood Falls. The upper portion of the Basswood River is considered "Dangerous Water." The 330-rod portage bypasses this section. It is the safest route, and I recommend it. If you prefer, however, you may flirt with the dangerous rapids by taking shorter portages instead of the one long one. Use your own discretion, based on the water conditions and your own skill. But keep these two historic facts in mind as you proceed: 1) many a foolish voyageur has lost his life on this portion of the Voyageurs' Highway trying to avoid the burdensome carries; and 2) as "Skipper" Berglund used to remind me, "No Indian ever lost his life on a portage."

You will find several nice campsites just below Lower Basswood Falls. Because of the heavy use of this area, you would be wise to get there as early as possible and make camp while sites are still available.

DAY 6: **Basswood River, Crooked Lake.** No need to put your boots on this morning. You won't encounter a single portage, just a LOT of paddling. A display of Indian rock paintings may be seen about a mile downstream from Lower Basswood Falls. Farther north, near the entrance to Wednesday Bay of Crooked Lake, you will pass Table Rock, a campsite long ago used by voyageurs carrying furs from the Northwest to outposts on Lake Superior. Keep your map handy on Crooked Lake. You will need it every minute! Watch for eagles soaring overhead: at least one nest is located near the east end.

DAY 7: **Crooked Lake,** p. 120 rods, **Iron Lake, Bottle Lake,** p. 80 rods, **Lac La Croix.** Curtain Falls, with a drop of 29 feet, separates Crooked and Iron lakes. Use caution and stay close to the left shoreline as you approach the misty brink of the beautiful falls. You will see at least three possible portage landings on the US shoreline, ranging from a couple hundred feet away from the falls to the very edge. It appears from the portage trail that a good many people prefer the second possible landing, several rods from the falls' edge.

When crossing Iron Lake, take time to go a short distance out of your way to visit Rebecca Falls, at the northern outlet into McAree Lake. (See comments for Day 5, Route #6.)

Two points of historical interest await you on Lac La Croix. Barely more than a mile past the portage from Bottle Lake is Warrior Hill, once the testing round for the bravery and strength of Ojibway braves, who ran from the lake's edge to the top of the rocky summit. If you climb to the top, you will be rewarded with an outstanding panorama of the surrounding area. Farther up the Canadian shoreline, you will soon come to a fine display of ancient Indian rock paintings. There are several outstanding campsites in the vicinity. Find one early, as this portion of the border is usually heavily traveled by motor boats and canoeists alike. The scenic splendor of this area makes the buzz of the motors tolerable.

DAY 8: **Lac La Croix,** p. 65 rods, **Boulder Bay,** p. 24 rods, **Lake Agnes,** p. 160 rods, **Oyster River,** p. 60 rods, **Oyster Lake.** If the water level is high enough and you prefer a few miles of extra paddling to eliminate 205 rods of portaging, you may wish to consider two alternatives. When leaving the south end of Lac La Croix, paddle past the 65-rod portage trail and continue through winding, shallow Boulder Bay to the 24-rod portage, into Lake Agnes. Then, instead of portaging 160-rods, to the Oyster River, exit Lake Agnes via the Nina-Moose River at the south end. Paddle upstream for half a mile to the mouth of the Oyster River on the right. You will soon come to a 20-rod portage, but the 160-rod one is not necessary.

DAY 9: **Oyster Lake,** p. 240 rods, **Hustler Lake,** p. 10 rods, **Ruby Lake,** p. 280 rods, **Lynx Lake,** p. 4 rods, **Little Shell Lake,** p. 10 rods, **Shell Lake.** Your first long portage is mostly uphill, climbing more than 140 feet above Oyster Lake. The 280-rod trail ascends very gradually, but then quickly drops nearly 130 feet to Lynx Lake. Be sure to safely elevate your food pack at night, as bears are a common nuisance around Shell Lake.

DAY 10: **Shell Lake,** p. 216 rods, **Lower Pauness Lake,** p. 8 rods, **Upper Pauness Lake, Little Indian Sioux River,** p. 60 rods, **river,** p. 40 rods, **Public Access.** If time permits you will surely enjoy a visit to Devil's Cascade, which plunges 75 feet down through a scenic granite gorge from Lower Pauness Lake to Loon Lake.

Entry Point 12—Little Vermillion Lake

Permits: 1105
Popularity Rank: 9
Daily Quota: 20

Location: Little Vermilion Lake is the westernmost entry point for the BWCA, located 40 miles northwest of Ely. It is accessible from popular Crane Lake, two miles to the west (five miles by water trails), at the north end of County Road 24. To get there from Ely, follow the Echo Trail 45 miles to its terminus and junction with County Road 24. Turn right and follow 24 north for 9 miles to the public access at the south end of Crane Lake. From Orr, Minnesota, drive east on County Road 23 for seventeen miles to the junction with County Road 24 at Buyck. Crane Lake is 13 miles north of Buyck on Co. 24.

Description: Public campgrounds are located near Orr and Buyck, and at Echo Lake, just east of the junction of the Echo Trail with County Road 24. The one at Echo Lake is the closest place to your trip's point of departure.

Although Little Vermilion Lake ranks high in popularity overall, only 11% of the summer use permits were issued to parties using canoes without motors. Most of the traffic consists of fishermen in motor boats on their way to ever-popular Lac La Croix, a Canadian border lake where motors are allowed by international agreement. Accordingly, you will find little peace and quiet during your first day on either of the suggested routes that follow. A major portion of each route, however, still maintains a high degree of wilderness character because it is beyond the popular motor routes leading to and along the Canadian border.

Wind can be a problem before you even reach Little Vermilion Lake, as both Crane and Sand Point lakes are highly susceptible to the effects of a strong northwest wind. Normally, however, winds are nearly calm early in the morning, when you will be crossing these two large lakes.

Crane Lake is well-populated with resorts and cabins along its southern shoreline. The north shore of Crane and the west shore of Sand Point mark the southeast boundary of the new Voyageurs National Park, which is another reason for Crane Lake's popularity.

Route #13: The Finger-Lac La Croix Loop

7 Days, 70 Miles, 16 Lakes, 1 River, 2 Creeks, 15 Portages
Difficulty: Challenging
Fisher map: 107

Introduction: This generally easy route takes you north from Crane to Sand Point Lake and then follows the international boundary south through Little Vermilion Lake and up the Loon River to Loon Lake. Continuing along the Canadian border, you will paddle north into beautiful Lac La Croix and follow this giant horseshoe for 25 miles north, then east, and then south to its very scenic southeastern corner. After viewing the Indian rock paintings and climbing to the top of legendary Warrior Hill, you will point back to the west and return to Loon Lake via the series of interesting lakes and streams that parallel the border a couple miles south of Lac La Croix. From Loon, you will retrace your path down the Loon River and through Little Vermilion Lake back to your origin at Crane Lake.

Although most of the route is easy, the series of frequent portages between Thumb and Little Loon lakes give this loop a rating of "Challenging." During the first half of the trip, only two portages will be encountered, but 13 of these obstacles will loom before you on your return trip from the southeast end of Lac La Croix. Water level should not be a critical factor on this route, except that very high water may necessitate a portage around "56 Rapids" on the Loon River. Finger and Pocket creeks could also be problems for heavily loaded canoes in very low water.

Most of this route is heavily used during summer months. Only that part between Pocket Creek and Little Loon Lake, which is the only part of the route where motors are prohibited, receives light-to-moderate use. Attractive scenery and several points of historical interest combine to compensate for the noise and congestion found along much of the route.

Anglers will find that northern pike predominate throughout most of the lakes on the loop. Walleye may also be found in Crane, Little Vermilion and Loon lakes, as well as in Lac La Croix, where lake trout and bass are also present.

DAY 1: **Crane Lake, Sand Point Lake, Little Vermilion Narrows, Little Vermilion Lake, Loon River,** p. 80 rods, **Loon Lake.** Because of the popularity of this motor route, and because Loon Lake is also accessible from another popular entry point, the Little Indian Sioux River — North, you will be wise to start your trip early so as to get one of the campsites on Loon Lake. If the wind cooperates, you should encounter no major obstacles this day, but it is a lot of paddling for a first day out!

DAY 2: **Loon Lake,** p. 50 rods, **Lac La Croix.** In the western half of Lac La Croix, you will see countless small islands that make navigation difficult at times. If necessary, use your compass to establish a general heading and forget about accounting for every little island you see, many of which are not even shown on the map. Don't miss the display of Indian rock paintings along the US shoreline, just north of the 50-rod "Beatty Portage" from Loon Lake. Along the Canadian shoreline, you will see a couple of resorts, and an Indian village farther east at the source of the Namakan River, in the Neguaguon Lake Indian Reservation, adjacent to Quetico Provincial Park. You should plan to spend the night somewhere near the northwest end of Coleman Island.

If you can make it a little farther, Lady Boot Bay offers a lovely setting in which to camp. One last note: **beware of sunburn.** On a day of continuous paddling, such as this one so early in your trip, it is very easy to absorb too many rays. Don't let it happen to you.

DAY 3: **Lac La Croix.** Because of the ever-present threat of wind on Lac La Croix, it is best to allow for two full days to paddle from one end to the other. A strong head wind is always a retarding menace, but also beware the strong TAIL wind. When starting across a wide-open expanse of water with a strong wind at your back, the lake ahead of you may appear to be quite safe. But, as you proceed farther and farther out from the shoreline or islands from which you were originally protected, you will find that the waves continue to build up, higher and higher, until suddenly you find your canoe swamped or capsized. Wind can be either a friend or a foe, depending on how much respect you have for it and how much good judgement you demonstrate in its presence.

Two fascinating points of historical interest await you in the southeast end of Lac La Croix. On the west shore of Canada's Irving Island, you will first pass another fine display of old Indian pictographs. About a mile further south, then, you will come to Warrior Hill, once the testing ground for the bravery and strength of Ojibway braves who ran from the lake's edge to the summit of the rocky precipice. You will be rewarded with an outstanding panorama of the surrounding area if you climb to the top. There are several outstanding campsites in the vicinity. Find one early, as this portion of border is still heavily traveled by motor boats and canoeists alike. The incredible beauty of this area makes the buzz of the motors tolerable.

You will find that Lady Boot Bay offers a lovely setting in which to camp this night. Several excellent campsites are also located near the pictographs.

DAY 4: **Lac La Croix, Pocket Creek,** p. 25 rods, **creek,** p. 20 rods, **Pocket Lake, Finger Creek,** p. 90 rods, **Finger Lake,** p. 9 rods, **Thumb Lake,** p. 200 rods, **Bear Track Lake.** All your portages this day are uphill, but none are difficult, including the 200-rod trail from Thumb to Bear Track, which follows a good path and has eight canoe rests along the way. You may be able to eliminate the 20-rod portage into Pocket Lake by paddling or walking your canoe up the shallow rapids draining Pocket Lake.

DAY 5: **Bear Track Lake,** p. 30 rods, **Little Bear Track Lake,** p. 50 rods, **Eugene Lake,** p. 45 rods, **Steep Lake,** p. 120 rods, **South Lake,** p. 72 rods, **Section 3 Pond,** p. 52 rods, **Slim Lake,** p. 173 rods, **Little Loon Lake, East Loon Bay.** The only uphill portage this day is the 72-rod trail from South Lake to Section 3 Pond. The 120-rod path out of Steep Lake is quite steep, but downhill.

DAY 6: **East Loon Bay, Loon Lake,** p. 80 rods, **Loon River, Little Vermilion Lake.** This day is short enough to allow plenty of time for a visit to one of area's most scenic attractions. Paddle to the far south end of Loon Lake, leave you canoe and gear at the base of the 160-rod portage, and hike up into the beautiful granite gorge through which Devil's Cascade plunges 75 feet from Lower Pauness Lake — a great place for a gorp break.

DAY 7: **Little Vermilion Lake, Little Vermilion Narrows, Sand Point Lake, Crane Lake.** This should all be familiar from your first day of paddling.

Route #14: The Iron-Horse-Hustler Route

12 Days, 130 Miles, 41 Lakes, 6 Rivers, 3 Creeks, 48 Portages
Difficulty: Challenging
Fisher maps: 107, 108, 112

Introduction: This scenic route will lead you to a smorgasbord of large and small lakes, winding little rivers and tiny creeks, half a dozen lively waterfalls and several points of historic interest. From Crane Lake you will first head north to Sand Point Lake, and then turn southeast and paddle along the Canadian border through Little Vermilion Lake and up the Loon River to Loon Lake. From East Loon Bay you will again travel north into a chain of small lakes and streams that lead east to the beautiful southeast end of giant Lac La Croix. Then, again you will follow the international boundary southeast through Iron and Crooked lakes and up the Basswood River, pausing to view lovely waterfalls en route. From Lower Basswood Falls you will leave the Land of the Maple Leaf and point your canoe southwest, up the placid Horse River to two popular fishing lakes, Horse and Fourtown. Paddling and portaging your way through another chain of small lakes, you'll plot a northwestward route that leads you down the Beartrap River and up Sterling Creek, eventually to Stuart Lake. From the west shore of Stuart Lake you will portage to the Dahlgren River and follow it down to the southernmost bay of Lac La Croix, only to jump quickly from it to Lake Agnes. From this heavily traveled lake, you will meander your way via the Oyster River to the part of the route that receives the least use by other canoeists. From Oyster, through Hustler and Lynx, to Lower Pauness Lake you will encounter many a long and arduous portage before re-entering familiar Loon Lake, where you camped the first night. From here on, you will backtrack down the Loon River and through Little Vermilion and Sand Point lakes to your origin at Crane Lake.

When finished, you will have seen virtually every kind of canoeing terrain in the BWCA. You will have seen two fine displays of old Indian rock paintings and several of the most scenic waterfalls in the Boundary Waters, and you will have had an excellent opportunity to see many of the species inhabiting the area: moose, deer, black bear, bald eagle, beaver and who knows what else.

While traveling along the Canadian border, where motors are allowed, you will doubtless see numerous other voyagers, as well as on Fourtown Lake and Lake Agnes. Along the rest of the route — the majority of it — however, you will see far fewer people and never hear the sound of a motor.

In addition to the fishing opportunities mentioned for Route #13, you will also find northern pike, walleye and pan fish in the border lakes, Horse, Fourtown and Agnes, and you might try for lake trout in Oyster Lake.

DAY 1: **Crane Lake, Sand Point Lake, Little Vermilion Narrows, Little Vermilion Lake, Loon River,** p. 80 rods, **Loon Lake.** (See comments for Day 1 of Route #13.)

DAY 2: **East Loon Bay, Little Loon Lake,** p. 173 rods, **Slim Lake,** p. 52 rods, **Section 3 Pond,** p. 72 rods, **South Lake,** p. 120 rods, **Steep Lake,** p. 45 rods, **Eugene Lake,** p. 50

rods, **Little Bear Track Lake,** p. 30 rods, **Bear Track Lake.**
Your first half-mile portage climbs about 65 feet from Little
Loon Lake to Slim Lake. It is steep in some places and muddy
in others, but five canoe rests along the way make the portaging a little easier. The one-third-mile portage into Steep Lake
climbs an exhausting 125 feet — perhaps the toughest portage
you'll run into until your last couple days.

DAY 3: **Bear Track Lake,** p. 200 rods, **Thumb Lake,** p. 9
rods, **Finger Lake,** p. 90 rods, **Finger Creek, Pocket Lake,**
p. 20 rods, **Pocket Creek,** p. 25 rods, **creek, Lac La Croix.** If
you wish, you can probably avoid the 20-rod portage out of
Pocket Lake by runnings, lining or walking your canoe down
the shallow rapids of Pocket Creek. Lac La Croix is the longest
and one of the most beautiful of the international lakes bordering the BWCA, dotted with over 200 rocky, picturesque
islands. Pocket Creek will lead you into the most scenic part of
the lake, and numerous good campsites are located near the
southeast end.

DAY 4: **Lac La Croix,** p. 80 rods, **Bottle Lake, Iron
Lake,** p. 120 rods, **Crooked Lake.** Before leaving Lac La
Croix in the morning, take time to explore the Indian rock
paintings and Warrior Hill found on the Canadian shoreline.
(See comments for Day 3 of Route #13.) Also take time, while
crossing Iron Lake, to visit Rebecca Ralls, at the outlet into
McAree Lake. (See comments for Day 5, Route #6.)

Curtain Falls, with a total drop of 29 feet, separates
Crooked and Iron lakes. Unlike Rebecca Falls, it will be approached from the bottom, and the portage around it is not
difficult.

DAY 5: **Crooked Lake, Basswood River,** Laced with
countless islands and protruding peninsulas, Crooked Lake
may be confusing to even an experienced guide. On an over-
cast day, a compass is mandatory. Watch overhead as you
wind your way through this fascinating lake, for at least one
bald-eagle nest is located near the east end, and eagles are
occasionally seen soaring above the lake. Between Wednesday
and Moose bays, you will paddle past Table Rock, a campsite
long ago popular among French-Canadian Voyageurs and
still used today. Three miles south of that point, you will pass
another good display of Indian pictographs. Several nice
campsites are located near the base of Lower Basswood Falls,
the final drop (12 feet) in the Basswood River.

DAY 6: **Basswood River,** p. 12 rods, **river, Horse
River,** p. 70 rods, **river,** p. 50 rods, **river, rapids, river,** p. 50
rods, **river, rapids, river, rapids, Horse Lake,** p. 70 rods,

pond p. 10 rods, **Fourtown Lake,** p. 1-3 rods, **Fourtown Lake,** p. 35 rods, **Boot Lake.** After your portage around Lower Basswood Falls and before entering the Horse River, you may enjoy paddling beyond this confluence to scenic Wheelbarrow Falls, about ¾ mile up the Basswood River, where the river drops another 12 feet.

While paddling up the Horse River, you will come to at least three short, shallow rapids, up which you will have to pull your canoe. These are located near the head of the river.

Horse and Fourtown Lakes are both BWCA entry lakes that are popular among fishermen. In them you will find northern pike, walleye and bluegill. Sea planes frequently bring fishermen to the south end of Fourtown, located outside the Boundary Waters, and motors are permitted throughout this lake. You will surely find camping much quieter on Boot Lake.

DAY 7: **Boot Lake,** p. 15 rods, **Fairy Lake,** p. 50 rods, **Gun Lake,** p. 30 rods, **Gull Lake,** p. 35 rods, **Mudhole Lake,** p. 55 rods, **Thunder Lake.** This will be an easy day, but since campsites are scarce between Thunder and Stuart lakes, it's best to stop here.

DAY 8: **Thunder Lake,** p. 9 rods, **Beartrap Lake,** p. 200 rods, **Beartrap River,** p. 160 rods, **river, Sunday Lake,** p. 8 rods, **Beartrap River, Sterling Creek, Sterling Lake,** p. 148 rods, **Bibon Lake,** p. 10 rods, **Nibin Lake,** p. 180 rods, **Stuart Lake.** The two big portages that confront you early this day are mostly downhill, descending nearly 100 feet in all between Beartrap Lake and Sunday Lake.

DAY 9: **Stuart Lake,** p. 118 rods, **Dahlgren River,** p. 140 rods, **Boulder Bay,** p. 24 rods, **Lake Agnes, Nina-Moose River, Oyster River,** p. 20 rods, **Oyster River,** p. 60 rods, **Oyster Lake.** If you are tired of river paddling by now, portage 160 rods from Lake Agnes to the Oyster River and eliminate a couple miles of paddling. Be sure to hang your food pack safely off the ground this night, as bears are known to raid campsites in this region.

DAY 10: **Oyster Lake,** p. 240 rods, **Hustler Lake,** p. 10 rods, **Ruby Lake,** p. 280 rods, **Lynx Lake,** p. 4 rods, **Little Shell Lake,** p. 10 rods, **Shell Lake.** Psych yourself up for the first long portage of the day, which is mostly uphill, climbing more than 140 feet above Oyster Lake. The 280-rod trail from Ruby Lake ascends very gradually, but then drops nearly 130 feet to Lynx Lake. Shell Lake is also in an area known for bear problems, so, again, be sure you elevate your food at night, and when you are away from camp.

DAY 11: **Shell Lake,** p. 216 rods, **Lower Pauness Lake,** p. 160 rods, **Loon Lake,** p. 80 rods, **Loon River, Little Vermilion Lake.** Your first long portage passes over a low ridge between Shell and Lower Pauness lakes, and it is not too difficult. The second is downhill, throughout a scenic granite gorge where Devil's Cascade plunges 75 feet from Lower Pauness Lake to Loon Lake. The third portage also bypasses a waterfall, where the Loon River drops 20 feet into Loon Lake. From that point on, you are back in what should be familiar territory.

DAY 12: **Little Vermilion Lake, Little Vermilion Narrows, Sand Point Lake, Crane Lake.** Welcome home!

Entry Point 14 — Little Indian Sioux River - North

Permits: 779
Popularity Rank: 13
Daily Quota: 8

   Location: The Little Indian Sioux River begins its winding course about 15 miles northwest of Ely. It flows west for about 6 miles and then turns north and eventually flows into Loon Lake on the Canadian border. All the river except that part in the immediate vicinity of the Echo Trail is contained within the BWCA. The upper part of the river (south of the Echo Trail) is accessible via the Sioux River-South entry point (#9), while the lower, northern part is served by the Sioux River-North entry point (#14). To get to the accesses, follow the Echo Trail for 28 miles from County Road 88. The North access begins at the *end* of the parking area just past the bridge, about a hundred rods north of the road.

   Description: A public campground at Jeanette Lake, 4 miles farther west on the Echo Trail, provides a good place to spend the night before your trip, enabling an early start the following morning.

   In spite of its remote location, this entry point is one of the more popular ones, providing easy access to beautiful, big Lac La Croix on the Canadian border. Although it is a designated motor route, 84% of the permits issued in 1977 were given to groups using canoes without motors. It seems that motorists aim for popular Lac La Croix through the easier Little Vermilion Lake entry point to the west.

   In addition to the two routes suggested below, you can also reverse Route #12 from the Little Indian Sioux River-South entry point (#9).

Route #15: The Pocket-Hustler Loop

6 Days, 60 Miles, 22 Lakes, 2 Rivers, 2 Creeks, 29 Portages
Difficulty: Challenging
Fisher map: 107

   Introduction: This circular loop begins with a portage and then follows the Little Indian Sioux River north to the Pauness lakes and on to Loon Lake on the Canadian border. It then turns east and follows a chain of fascinating little lakes and streams that parallel the Canadian border seldom more than 2 miles south of the international boundary. You will

Portage between Seagull and Saganaga Lakes

A beaver palace in the Moose River

Portaging from Big Moose Lake to Duck Lake

The Painted Rocks on Lac La Croix   *George Miles Ryan*

Lunch break beside the Kawashiwi River

Lower Basswood Falls tempted many a foolish Voyageur

Paddling up the Moose River toward Big Moose Lake

Curtain Falls between Crooked Lake and Iron Lake

Walking the Kawashiwi River rapids

Basswood River   *Donald Holmquist*

Agamak Lake

Minnesota Tourist Bureau

Putting in at Duck Lake

then enter the scenic southeast end of Lac La Croix, where you will have an opportunity to view old Indian rock paintings and climb legendary Warrior Hill. From the southeast tip of this mammoth lake, you will portage into Lake Agnes and then turn west through a series of rugged portages connecting lakes used less than any others on this route. Through Oyster, Hustler and Shell lakes, you will re-enter the Pauness lakes and then retrace your path up the Little Indian Sioux River to your origin at the Echo Trail.

Motors are prohibited on most of the lakes and streams on this route. However, Lac La Croix is often buzzing with traffic from an Indian village and two resorts located along its north shore. Nevertheless, its scenic beauty more than compensates for these sounds of civilization. The region south of Lac La Croix, where most of this route lies, receives generally light use, and you will have little or no competition for campsites during all but the busiest summer periods.

Fishing is good for northern pike in most of the lakes on this route. Anglers will also find walleye along the way, particularly in Loon and Agnes lakes and Lac La Croix. Lake trout also inhabit the depths of Oyster Lake and Lac La Croix.

DAY 1: Portage 40 rods, **Little Indian Sioux River,** p. 60 rods, **river, Upper Pauness Lake,** p. 8 rods, **Lower Pauness Lake,** p. 160 rods, **Loon Lake, East Loon Bay.** A great place to eat lunch on your first day is at Devil's Cascade, which plunges 75 feet through a scenic granite gorge from Lower Pauness Lake to Loon Lake. There are several good campsites on Loon Lake, but those in East Loon Bay may offer a little more peace than those near the motor route to Lac La Croix.

DAY 2: **East Loon Bay, Little Loon Lake,** p. 173 rods, **Slim Lake,** p. 52 rods, **Section 3 pond,** p. 72 rods, **South Lake,** p. 120 rods, **Steep Lake,** p. 45 rods, **Eugene Lake,** p. 50 rods, **Little Bear Track Lake,** p. 30 rods, **Bear Track Lake.** As the crow flies, you are not going far this day, but there's a lot of walking along the way! Your first portage of over half a mile climbs about sixty-five feet from Little Loon Lake to Slim Lake. It is steep in some places and muddy in others, but five canoe rests along the way make portaging a LITTLE easier. The one-third mile portage into Steep Lake climbs an exhausting 125 feet — perhaps the toughest portage during the first half of the route.

DAY 3: **Bear Track Lake,** p. 200 rods, **Thumb Lake,** p. 9 rods, **Finger Lake,** p. 90 rods, **Finger Creek, Pocket Lake,** p. 20 rods, **Pocket Creek,** p. 25 rods, **creek, Lac La Croix.** If you wish, you can probably avoid the 20-rod portage out of

Pocket Lake by running, lining or walking the shallow rapids of Pocket Creek. Pocket Creek will lead you into the most scenic part of Lac La Croix, and numerous good campsites are located near the southeast end. Take time to explore the Indian rock paintings and Warrior Hill on the Canadian shoreline. (See comments for Day 6, Route #10.)

DAY 4: **Lac La Croix,** p. 65 rods, **Boulder Bay,** p. 24 rods, **Lake Agnes,** p. 160 rods, **Oyster River,** p. 60 rods, **Oyster Lake.** (See comments for Day 8, Route #12.)

DAY 5: **Oyster Lake,** p. 240 rods, **Hustler Lake,** p. 10 rods, **Ruby Lake,** p. 280 rods, **Lynx Lake,** p. 4 rods, **Little Shell Lake,** p. 10 rods, **Shell Lake.** (See comments for Day 9, Route #12.)

DAY 6: **Shell Lake,** p. 216 rods, **Lower Pauness Lake,** p. 8 rods, **Upper Pauness Lake, Little Indian Sioux River,** p. 60 rods, **river,** p. 40 rods, **Public Access.** Your first portage this day is long, but not too difficult, as it passes over a low ridge between Shell and Lower Pauness Lake. From that point on you will be backtracking on your first day's path.

Route #16: Crooked-Beartrap Loop

9 Days, 84 Miles, 28 Lakes, 4 Rivers, 7 Creeks, 35 Portages
Difficulty: Challenging
Fisher maps: 107, 108

Introduction: This Canadian border route actually deserves TWO difficulty ratings: EASY for the first half, RUGGED for the second half. From the parking lot north of the Echo Trail, you will first portage 40 rods to the Little Indian Sioux River and then follow that winding, slow stream north through the Pauness lakes to the international boundary at Loon Lake. Continuing north, you will enter ever-popular Lac La Croix and follow this giant horseshoe first north, then east, and finally south to its most beautiful southeast part. While paddling the length of this 25-mile-lake, you will view two displays of Indian pictographs and a thriving Indian village and climb the legendary Warrior Hill. You will continue paddling southeast along the international boundary through Bottle and Iron lakes, portage around scenic Curtain Falls, and enter the maze of peninsulas and islands in Crooked Lake. From Friday Bay of Crooked Lake, you will then turn south and traverse a series of much smaller lakes and their interconnecting streams to Gun Lake. Turning northwest here, you will follow the Beartrap River down to Sterling Creek and then head west to Stuart Lake. After a brief return to Lac La

Croix, at its southernmost bay, you will continue west through a series of lightly traveled lakes and rugged portages back to the Pauness lakes, and then retrace your path up the Little Indian Sioux River to your origin at the Echo Trail.

During the first half of this trip, nearly all your energy will be expended in paddling. From the beginning to the northeasternmost point in this loop, only seven portages are encountered. But you will cross 28 on your return trip, many of which are over ½ mile in length! Wind and large waves are a constant threat on the open expanses of Lac La Croix, and an ever-present menace along much of the Canadian border. Although wind is of little concern along the bottom half of this loop, water level is — particularly on the Beartrap, Dahlgren and Oyster rivers. Be prepared for additional walking during periods of low water.

Fishermen, resort visitors and the residents of a nearby Indian village all operate motorboats on Lac La Croix. And all the other border lakes, too, are heavily used during most of the summer. But the second half of this loop is through a part of the BWCA that is lightly used throughout most of the summer, and motors are prohibited from all the lakes here except Agnes.

Anglers will find northern pike and walleye in many of the lakes on this route. And for those who like to WORK for their dinner, you will find lake trout inhabiting the depths of Lac La Croix and Oyster Lake.

DAY 1: P. 40 rods, **Little Indian Sioux River,** p. 60 rods, **river, Upper Pauness Lake,** p. 8 rods, **Lower Pauness Lake,** p. 160 rods, **Loon Lake.** (See comments for Day 1, Route #15.)

DAY 2: **Loon Lake,** p. 50 rods, **Lac La Croix.** (See comments for Day 2, Route #13.)

DAY 3: **Lac La Croix.** (See comments for Day 3, Route #13.)

DAY 4: **Lac La Croix,** p. 80 rods, **Bottle Lake, Iron Lake,** p. 120 rods, **Crooked Lake.** (See comments for Day 5, Route #6.)

DAY 5: **Crooked Lake (Friday Bay),** p. 95 rods, **Pappoose Creek, Pappoose Lake, creek,** p. 5 rods, **creek, Chippewa Lake, creek, Niki Lake,** p. 45 rods, **Wagosh Lake,** p. 300 rods, **Gun Lake.** During periods of very low water, you may also have to portage 42 rods between Chippewa and Niki lakes. The last two portages this day are exhausting. The 45-rod trail from Niki Lake to Wagosh Lake may be short, but it is steep, gaining 73 feet in elevation before

decending 6 feet to Wagosh. The 300-rod path from Wagosh to
Gun, in turn, surmounts a 117-foot hill and returns to nearly
the same elevation at which it started.

DAY 6: **Gun Lake,** p. 30 rods, **Gull Lake,** p. 35 rods,
Mudhole Lake, p. 55 rods, **Thunder Lake,** p. 9 rods,
Beartrap Lake, p. 200 rods, **Beartrap River,** p. 160 rods,
river, Sunday Lake, p. 8 rods, **Beartrap River, Sterling
Creek, Sterling Lake.** The two big portages that confront you
this day are predominantly downhill, descending nearly 100
feet in all between Beartrap Lake and Sunday Lake. Since
campsites are somewhat at a premium in this area, you may
wish to stop early on Sunday Lake, or you may have to continue past Sterling to Bibon or Nibin Lake.

DAY 7: **Sterling Lake,** p. 148 rods, **Bibon Lake,** p. 10
rods, **Nibin Lake,** p. 180 rods, **Stuart Lake,** p. 118 rods,
Dahlgren River, p. 140 rods, **Boulder Bay,** p. 24 rods, **Lake
Agnes.** Although most of this day will be spent in an area of
light use, you will find yourself camping on a lake receiving
heavy use as part of a popular motor route from the Moose
River to Lac La Croix. Many good campsites are located here,
but there are also many parties competing for them, as this
lake is a popular first stop for those beginning their trips
through the Moose River entry point. Be sure to hang your
food safely off the ground at night, as bears frequent the area.

DAY 8: **Lake Agnes,** p. 160 rods, **Oyster River,** p. 60
rods, **Oyster Lake,** p. 240 rods, **Hustler Lake,** p. 10 rods,
Ruby Lake, p. 280 rods, **Lynx Lake.** (See comments for Days
8 and 9, Route #12.)

DAY 9: **Lynx Lake,** p. 4 rods, **Little Shell Lake,** p. 10
rods, **Shell Lake,** p. 216 rods, **Lower Pauness Lake,** p. 8
rods, **Upper Pauness Lake, Little Indian Sioux River,** p.
60 rods, **river,** p. 40 rods, **Public Access.** The long portage of
this day passes over a low ridge between Shell Lake and Lower
Pauness Lake, and it is not difficult. From that point on, you
will be backtracking on your first day's path.

Entry Point 16—Moose River

Permits: 934
Popularity Rank: 12
Daily Quota: 9

    Location: The Moose River begins its course at the northwest corner of Big Moose Lake, 15 miles northwest of Ely, and slowly winds its way north for about 10 miles to Nina-Moose Lake. The Echo Trail crosses the river about 4 miles south of Nina-Moose Lake. To get to the public access, follow the Echo Trail 22 miles from County Road 88. Just before the road crosses the river, an access road spurs off to the north (right). Follow it for 1 mile to the public parking lot and portage trail to the Moose River. (Note: About a mile before this spur, you will see a sign pointing to the Moose River via Forest Route 464, south of the Echo Trail. Do not turn here; this road leads to the access serving the Big Moose Lake entry point.)

    Description: The Fenske Lake Campground, 16 miles toward Ely on the Echo Trail, offers a good place to spend the night before your trip. There is also a National Forest campground 10 miles farther west on the Echo Trail, at Lake Jeanette.

    For the purpose of "visitor distribution" the Moose River entry point is grouped with the Portage River (#17) and Blandin Road (#11) entry points. Only 11 travel permits may be issued each day for all three combined. Of the three, the Moose River is by far the most popular entry point, and the most suitable for canoeists. Therefore, it is the only one of the three chosen for inclusion in this book.

    The Moose River is quite narrow and shallow, it meanders considerably, and it is almost choked with vegetation for the first few miles. Although it is a designated motor route, man-powered canoes far outnumber those propelled by motors. In fact, 83% of the travel permits issued in 1977 went to groups using canoes without motors. The Moose is a pretty little river that you are sure to enjoy.

Route #17: The Iron-Duck Loop

5 Days, 43 Miles, 12 Lakes, 4 Rivers, 27 Portages
Difficulty: Rugged
Fisher maps: 107, 112

    Introduction: This winding route will take you through

the entire length of three rivers and the first part of a fourth.
In fact, most of your time will be spent on these rivers, with
frequent portages thrown in to stretch your muscles, including five carries of over ½ mile in length.

You start right off with one of those portages — 160 rods
from the Moose River parking lot to your first "taste" of the
Moose River. You will paddle north down this lazy stream to
Nina-Moose Lake, and then continue north down the Nina-
Moose River to Lake Agnes. After two short portages to the
north, you will be on big, beautiful Lac La Croix, which constitutes 25 miles of our international boundary. You will follow the border southeast to Iron Lake and then turn south
through a series of tiny lakes to Stuart Lake. Continuing
south, you will paddle up the Stuart River, portage nearly 2
miles across the Echo Trail, and find your campsite on Big
Lake, situated outside the BWCA. From Big Lake you will
paddle and portage your way southwest to Big Moose Lake
and then re-enter the Moose River, which will, of course, bring
you back to your origin at the Moose River parking lot.

If the water level is low, find another route. This one is
best during periods of higher water. Fishing is fairly good for
walleye, northern pike and bass in most of the lakes on this
route. Lake trout are also found in Lac La Croix.

During your brief visit to the Canadian border, you will
have an opportunity to view two scenic waterfalls, a good
display of old Indian rock paintings and an outstanding
panorama from atop legendary Warrior Hill. All this and
more in a five-day flurry that you won't soon forget!

DAY 1: P. 160 rods, **Moose River,** p. 20 rods, **river,** p. 25
rods, **river, Nina-Moose Lake, Nina-Moose River,** p. 70
rods, **river,** p. 96 rods, **river, Lake Agnes.** Small beaver dams
sometimes pop up on slow streams like these. You may have
an occasional quick liftover in addition to the portages
mentioned. On the west shore of Nina-Moose Lake you will see
evidence of the 1971 fire that ravaged 25 square miles of
woodland between here and the Little Indian Sioux River.

DAY 2: **Lake Agnes,** p. 24 rods, **Boulder Bay,** p. 65 rods,
Lac La Croix, p. 80 rods, **Bottle Lake, Iron Lake.** If you
prefer a couple of extra miles of paddling to a 65-rod portage,
follow the shallow, meandering course of Boulder Bay from
the 24-rod portage to Lac La Croix. And, before leaving it to
the east you may wish to paddle an extra mile and a half north
to two points of historic interest. On the granite cliffs of the
Canadian shoreline are the fading red-brown remnants of
pictographs long ago painted by the Ojibway Indians who

inhabited the area. About a mile to the south is a high, rock-faced hill that was once the testing ground for the bravery and strength of Ojibway braves who ran from the lake's edge to the summit. It is known as Warrior Hill. You will find an out-standing vista after a climb to the top.

Before leaving Iron Lake, be sure to visit two of the most scenic natural attractions in this part of the BWCA — Rebecca Falls, and Curtain Falls. (See comments for Day 5, Route #6.)

DAY 3: **Iron Lake,** p. 72 rods, **Dark Lake,** p. 67 rods, **Rush Lake,** p. 60 rods, **Fox Lake,** p. 320 rods, **Stuart Lake.** The short portages south of Iron Lake require some steep climbing, but they are short enough to cause no major difficulty. The mile trek to Stuart Lake is slightly downhill along most of its course. Although you should arrive early at Stuart Lake, it is best to go no farther, as there are no Forest Service campsites along the Stuart River.

DAY 4: **Stuart Lake,** p. 80 rods, **Stuart River,** p. 8 rods, **river,** p. 14 rods, **river,** p. 74 rods, **river,** p. 30 rods, **river,** p. 95 rods, **river,** p. 600 rods, **Big Lake.** All the portages this long day are in general uphill, as you will be paddling *up* this meandering, marshy stream. Your last carry is the longest portage on this route — nearly 2 miles — and it crosses the Echo Trail about 85 rods from the south end.

DAY 5: **Big Lake, Portage River,** p. 150 rods, **Duck Lake,** p. 480 rods, **Big Moose Lake,** p. 60 rods, **Moose River,** p. 160 rods, **river,** p. 17 rods, **river,** p. 40 rods, **river,** p. 40 rods, **river,** p. 77 rods, **Moose River parking lot.** This is another rough day of long portages and slow river travel. You could shorten it by having a vehicle waiting at the Moose River access from Forest Route 464. This would eliminate about 4 miles of meandering and four short portages through a portion of the route not contained in the BWCA.

Route #18: The Slim-Indian Sioux Route

8 Days, 85 Miles, 21 Lakes, 4 Rivers, 2 Creeks, 44 Portages
Difficulty: Challenging
Fisher maps: 107, 111, 112

Introduction: Like Route #17, this high-quality wilderness route follows rivers for much of its course. From the Moose River parking lot you will paddle down the winding Moose and Nina-Moose rivers, through Lake Agnes to Lac La Croix, an international border lake where fishermen and motorboats are common. But you will soon leave the busy motor route, enter peaceful Pocket Creek and traverse the chain of small lakes and tiny streams west to Slim Lake. Turning south then, you will again touch the Canadian border on popular Loon Lake before continuing south through the Pauness lakes and up the Little Indian Sioux River to the Echo Trail. You will portage past this popular entry point and continue up the Sioux River, entering a part of the Boundary Waters seldom visited by other canoeists. Along its sluggish, meandering course, you will have an excellent opportunity to view moose, deer, beaver and other forms of wildlife before entering Otter and Cummings lakes. From Cummings Lake you will carry your gear across the longest portage on this route, to Big Moose Lake, and then follow the Moose River again, down its winding course to your origin at the Moose River parking lot.

When finished, you will have seen a good display of Indian rock paintings, an awesome panorama from atop Warrior Hill, the impressive Devil's Cascade, and, most likely, countless forms of North Woods fauna. The part of this route north of the Echo Trail receives moderate-to-heavy use during much of the summer, but the region south of the road has been seen by few other visitors to the Boundary Waters. You will quickly sense the pristine character of the Sioux River, and here you will experience as much solitude and isolation as you could hope to find anywhere in the BWCA.

Northern pike inhabit the waters throughout most of the route. You will also find walleye and bass in Agnes, Nina-Moose and Loon Lake, as well as in Lac La Croix, where lake trout may also be caught.

Water level is a critical factor on this route. The Little Indian Sioux River, in particular, may be too dry for navigation during especially dry years, or during the dry periods of a typical summer. Late spring or early summer, or after the autumn rains, is usually the best time for this trip.

DAY 1: P. 160 rods, **Moose River,** p. 20 rods, **river,** p. 25 rods, **river, Nina-Moose Lake, Nina-Moose River,** p. 70 rods, **river,** p. 96 rods, **river, Lake Agnes.** (See comments for Day 1, Route #17.)

DAY 2: **Lake Agnes,** p. 24 rods, **Boulder Bay,** p. 65 rods, **Lac La Croix.** (See comments for Day 2, Route #17.) You'll find several good campsites in and north of Lady Boot Bay, near the mouth of Pocket Creek.

DAY 3: **Lac La Croix, Pocket Creek,** p. 25 rods, **creek,** p. 20 rods, **Pocket Lake, Finger Creek,** p. 90 rods, **Finger Lake,** p. 9 rods, **Thumb Lake,** p. 200 rods, **Bear Track Lake,**

p. 30 rods, **Little Bear Track Lake,** p. 50 rods, **Eugene Lake.**
Your first five portages this day are uphill, but none is difficult, including the 200-rod trail from Thumb to Bear Track,
which follows a good path and has eight canoe rests along the
way. You may be able to eliminate the 20-rod portage into
Pocket Lake by paddling or walking your canoe up the shallow
rapids draining Pocket Lake.

   DAY 4: **Eugene Lake,** p. 45 rods, **Steep Lake,** p. 120
rods, **South Lake,** p. 72 rods, **Section Three Pond,** p. 52 rods,
Slim Lake, p. 173 rods, **Little Loon Lake, East Loon Bay,
Loon Lake,** p. 160 rods, **Lower Pauness Lake.** The 120-rod
path out of Steep Lake is quite steep, but fortunately downhill.
The only major uphill trek of the day is the half-mile portage
around Devil's Cascade, south of Loon Lake. When you have
completed this task, reward yourself by hiking back down into
this scenic granite gorge and viewing the progression of
waterfalls and rapids plunging 75 feet from Lower Pauness
Lake to Loon Lake. Plan to camp early this evening, as the
Pauness lakes are a popular first-night stop for those getting a
late start from the Little Indian Sioux River — North entry
point.

   DAY 5: **Lower Pauness Lake,** p. 8 rods, **Upper Pauness Lake, Little Indian Sioux River,** p. 60 rods, **river,** p.
120 rods, **river,** p. 8 rods, **river,** p. 120 rods, **river, Little Pony
River,** p. 60 rods, **river,** p. 60 rods, **Bootleg Lake.** The Little
Indian Sioux River is another slow, shallow, meandering
stream, fairly wide in its lower reaches, but becoming nar-
rower the farther up stream you get, until it is wide enough
only for single-file canoeing as you approach its source. Moose
and deer are common sights along its marshy banks. Strong
head winds can slow your progress considerably.

   When you begin your 120-rod portage across the Echo
Trail, follow the less-used trail nearest the river. The more
trodden path on the right leads for 40 rods to the Sioux River
parking lot. Although you could take this route, it is longer
than need be.

   DAY 6: **Bootleg Lake,** p. 200 rods, **Little Indian Sioux
River,** p. 40 rods, **river,** p. 35 rods, **river,** p. 20 rods, **river,** p.
30 rods, **river,** p. 40 rods, **river,** p. 20 rods, **river,** p. 28 rods,
river, p. 120 rods, **Otter Lake,** p. 5 rods, **Cummings Lake.**
Because of the constant winding and the numerous short
portages, travel is deceivingly slow on the supper part of the
Sioux River. There are no designated Forest Service campsites
along the river, and very few places that are even possible for
camping along this swampy stream. So it is important that

you forge onward to Cummings Lake before dusk, where several good campsites await your selection.

DAY 7: **Cummings Lake,** p. 580 rods, **Big Moose Lake.** As the crow flies, you won't be going far this day, but you'll feel like you have at day's end! Your longest carry of the trip will occupy a good deal of your time, especially if you are unable to transport all your gear in one trip. In spite of its length, the portage is not too difficult. Except for a few small hills at each end, the trail follows a rather level ridge much of the way, and 19 canoe rests are situated at regular intervals along its course. If you can take your mind off the heavy cargo on your shoulders, you will find the scenery to be quite lovely along the trail.

DAY 8: **Big Moose Lake,** p. 60 rods, **Moose River,** p. 160 rods, **river,** p. 17 rods, **river,** p. 40 rods, **river,** p. 40 rods, **river,** p. 77 rods, **river, Moose River parking lot.** What would be a more appropriate end to this meandering trip than another winding little river?

Entry Point 19—Stuart River

Permits: 92
Popularity Rank: 49
Daily Quota: 1

   Location: The headwaters of the Stuart River are about 15 miles northwest of Ely, just north of Big Lake. The swampy, little river flows slowly northward for about 6 miles to Stuart Lake, 4 miles south of the Canadian border. Access to the river is across a 513-rod portage from the Echo Trail, 17 miles northwest of County Road 88.

   Description: A National Forest campground at Fenske Lake, 9 miles closer to Ely on the Echo Trail, is a good place to spend the night before your trip. This enables you to get an early start the following morning — and you will need it.

   The long access portage to the river is mostly downhill, but it's a rugged way to start any trip. Beyond it, you will find no designated campsites along the tiny, shallow river — not until persistent paddling and six more portages have taken you into Stuart Lake. Motors are not allowed on this river, and few canoes utilize it. Consequently, this BWCA access point offers a quick entrance into the kind of pristine wilderness that might take several days to find from many other entry points.

Route #19: Five Rivers Route

4 Days, 35 Miles, 7 Lakes, 5 Rivers, 24 Portages
Difficulty: Rugged
Fisher maps: 107, 112

   Introduction: After the first gruelling portage from the Echo Trail, this river-running route will take you north down the lazy Stuart River to Stuart Lake. You will then portage onto the Dahlgren River and follow it northwest to Boulder Bay on Lac La Croix. Then you will head south into Lake Agnes and up the Nina-Moose River to Nina-Moose Lake. Continuing south, you will paddle up your fourth winding stream, the Moose River, under the Echo Trail to Big Moose Lake. From the east side of this beautiful, large lake, you will portage 1½ miles into Duck Lake and another ⅓ miles to the Portage River, which carries you into Big Lake, a short portage away from your origin at the Echo Trail. Although you will be camping only on lakes, you'll be paddling almost exclusively on rivers for the first three days of this trip. Accordingly, water level is an important consideration. The Stuart River and the upper portion of the Moose River, in particular, could provide difficult passage during dry periods. Normally, therefore, spring and early summer, as well as after the fall rains, are the best times to take this loop.

Motors are prohibited from most of the route. Only in the stretch from Lake Agnes to the Moose River Parking Lot, where moderate use occurs, are they allowed. Elsewhere use is light.

For anglers, walleye, northern pike and smallmouth bass prevail throughout much of the route.

DAY 1: P. 513 rods, **Stuart River,** p. 95 rods, **river,** p. 30 rods, **river,** p. 74 rods, **river,** p. 14 rods, **river,** p. 8 rods, **river,** p. 80 rods, **Stuart Lake.** If you should get a late start and Stuart Lake is too far for the first night, there is a campsite on White Feather Lake, accessible through a short stream that connects to the Stuart River just south of the 74-rod portage.

DAY 2: **Stuart Lake,** p. 118 rods, **Dahlgren River,** p. 140 rods, **Boulder Bay,** p. 24 rods, **Lake Agnes, Nina-Moose River,** p. 96 rods, **river,** p. 70 rods, **river, Nina-Moose Lake.** You will probably see the most people this day, as you travel up the popular motor route from the Moose River entry point. So try to find a campsite early on busy Nina-Moose Lake. Along the west shore of this lake you will see scars of the great fire of 1971 that ravaged nearly 25 square miles of woodland between here and the Little Indian Sioux River.

DAY 3: **Nina-Moose Lake, Moose River,** p. 25 rods, **river,** p. 20 rods, **river,** p. 160 rods, **river,** p. 77 rods, **river,** p. 40 rods, **river,** p. 40 rods, **river,** p. 17 rods, **river,** p. 160 rods, **river,** p. 60 rods, **Big Moose Lake.** (See comments for Day 8, Route #10.)

DAY 4: **Big Moose Lake,** p. 480 rods, **Duck Lake,** p. 150 rods, **Portage River, Big Lake,** p. 87 rods. You will be outside the BWCA all of this day, but few if any other people will share your route, in spite of the location of two resorts on Big Lake.

Route #20: The Beartrap-Range Rivers Route

7 Days, 55 Miles, 30 Lakes, 4 Rivers, 2 Creeks, 42 Portages
Difficulty: Rugged
Fisher maps: 107, 108, 112

Introduction: This is another loop through a part of the BWCA that receives light-to-moderate use most of the summer. From the Echo Trail, you will portage 513 rods to the

Stuart River and then follow it north to the portage into Nibin Lake. After paddling through Nibin and Bibon lakes and down Sterling Creek, you will soon meet the Beartrap River and follow it southeast to its headwaters at Beartrap Lake. Continuing southeast, you will paddle and portage your way through a chain of popular fishing lakes to the Range River. This shallow, marshy creek will lead you southwest to the Grassy River and on to Grassy Lake. From Grassy Lake you will pass through a chain of small, picturesque lakes, cross the Echo Trail and eventually go onto the North Arm of big Burntside Lake, a populated lake just outside the BWCA. After portaging across County Road 644, you will re-enter the Boundary Waters and travel through one of the least used portions in the BWCA, between Slim and Big lakes. At the north end of Big Lake you will find the portage that takes you back to your origin at the Echo Trail.

Motors are prohibited on most of this route, except on Fourtown Lake and on those lakes outside of the Boundary Waters. Elsewhere, you will surely find a high-quality wilderness setting, with lovely scenery and plentiful wildlife. Nearly all the route will be on narrow rivers, winding creeks and small lakes. Walleye, northern pike and pan fish prevail.

Because rivers are a major portion of the loop, water level plays an important role in the suitability of this route. During especially dry periods, the Stuart and Range rivers, in particular, may be too low for navigation.

DAY 1: P. 513 rods, **Stuart River,** p. 95 rods, **river,** p. 30 rods, **river,** p. 74 rods, **river,** p. 14 rods, **river,** p. 8 rods, **river,** p. 100 rods, **Nibin Lake.** (See comments for Route #19, Day 1) If the campsite on Nibin Lake is taken, you should consider a side trip to Stuart Lake, where sites are more plentiful, rather than continuing east, where sites continue to be scarce. But, then, this means over a mile of additional portaging.

DAY 2: **Nibin Lake,** p. 10 rods, **Bibon Lake,** p. 148 rods, **Sterling Lake, Sterling Creek, Beartrap River,** p. 8 rods, **Sunday Lake, Beartrap River,** p. 160 rods, **river,** p. 200 rods, **Beartrap Lake,** p. 9 rods, **Thunder Lake.** You will be portaging mostly uphill this day, climbing a hundred feet from Sunday Lake to Beartrap Lake.

DAY 3: **Thunder Lake,** p. 55 rods, **Mudhole Lake,** p. 35 rods, **Gull Lake,** p. 30 rods, **Gun Lake,** p. 50 rods, **Fairy Lake,** p. 15 rods, **Boot Lake,** p. 35 rods, **Fourtown Lake,** p. 1-3 rods, **Fourtown Lake,** p. 10 rods, **pond,** p. 70 rods, **Horse Lake.** Fourtown Lake is a popular "fly-in" point of departure for fishermen. And, although the surrounding lakes are "pad-

dle only", Fourtown, itself, is open to motorboats. Consequently, you may find this portion of your trip to be a rather
noisy change of pace from the prior two-and-a-half days of
peaceful paddling.

DAY 4: **Horse Lake,** p. 90 rods, **Tin Can Lake,** p. 340
rods, **Range Lake, Range River,** p. 10 rods, **river,** p. 30 rods,
river, p. 1 rod, **river, Grassy River,** p. 24 rods, **Beaver Pond,
Grassy Lake.** The long portage from Tin Can to Range Lake
may be split into two portages of 160 rods each, if you prefer,
with a short interconnecting paddle on Sandpit Lake. Either
way, the portage is not rough. It follows an old railroad bed
that once served logging operations in the area. Don't be
surprised to see a couple of beaver dams obstructing the Range
River. The 1-rod portage is merely a liftover, where the
Cloquet Road crosses the river. If the water level is low, there
may be another short portage between the beaver pond and
Grassy Lake. (See detailed sketch of Range River region in
Route #8.)

DAY 5: **Grassy Lake,** p. 48 rods, **Tee Lake,** p. 120 rods,
Sletten Lake, p. 70 rods, **Little Sletten Lake,** p. 10 rods,
Fenske Lake, p. 120 rods, **Everett Lake,** p. 14 rods, **East
Twin Lake, West Twin Lake.** Take your time this day, and
enjoy the scenic appeal of the tiny lakes on which you are
traveling — as lovely as any portion of the route in the BWCA.
Your first two portages are entirely uphill, and the third is
over a small hill. But from there on, it is easy going all the way
to West Twin Lake. You will cross the Echo Trail near the end
of the 120-rod portage from Fenske to Everett Lake.

DAY 6: **West Twin Lake,** p. 250 rods, **North Arm of
Burntside Lake,** p. 140 rods, **Slim Lake,** p. 77 rods, **Rice
Lake,** p. 130 rods, **Hook Lake.** If the time is right, you will
have a good opportunity to pick enough blueberries this day
for a pie, pancakes, muffins, and other concoctions. At the end
of the portage to Slim Lake is a trail off to the right that leads
up to a rock cliff that abounds with berry bushes. If high,
scenic lookouts thrill you, take the time to paddle out of your
way to the south end of Slim Lake and hike to Old Baldy. (See
comments for Day 1, Route #7.)

DAY 7: **Hook Lake,** p. 520 rods, **Big Rice Lake,** p. 8 rods,
Big Rice Creek, Lapond Lake, p. 150 rods, **Big Lake,** p. 87
rods. This part of the BWCA is seldom visited, except for the
immediate vicinity of Big Lake. Your first portage is certainly
long enough, but not difficult. You will find two resorts on the
north shore of Big Lake, should you wish to satisfy any crav-
ings for "civilized" food or drink.

Entry Point 21 — Fourtown Lake

Permits: 308
Popularity Rank: 28
Daily Quota: 2

Location: Fourtown Lake is accessible from Nels Lake, located almost 9 miles straight north of Ely. To get there, follow County Road 116 (Echo Trail) north and west from County Road 88 for 10 miles, ¾ miles past the intersection with County Road 644. As the Echo Trail bends to the left, a one-lane primitive road branches to the right (east). Follow this narrow, winding path for ¾ mile to Nels Lake, where a small parking lot is adjacent to the public landing.

Description: Camping is prohibited at the landing, but a Forest Service campsite is located nearby on the lake, with a path leading to it from the landing. If it is occupied or inconvenient, you may wish to spend the night before your trip at Fenske Lake Campground, 2 miles closer to Ely on the Echo Trail.

The three lakes leading to Fourtown Lake and the southern portion of Fourtown itself are outside the Boundary Waters Canoe Area, and motor travel, cans and bottles are not prohibited at them. But you won't see many motor boats (or canoes, for that matter) between Nels and Fourtown. Instead, you will see and hear float planes frequently landing on the southern end of Fourtown, depositing and withdrawing fishermen and canoeists who prefer to pay for such luxury rather than endure the six portages between Nels and Fourtown lakes. Although Fourtown is a fairly active motor-designated lake, the neighboring lakes are "paddle only" and rather lightly traveled.

In spite of the proximity of Horse Lake, Fourtown and Horse are designated as two separate entry points. Consequently if you find the Fourtown entry point "closed" on the day when your trip is scheduled, you can take virtually the same route by entering the BWCA through Horse Lake (#22) instead. Similarly, if both entry points are closed, you can reverse Route #21 by entering the BWCA through the Range River (#23). See #22 — Horse Lake for other route ideas in this area.

Route #21: Three Falls Loop

3 Days, 37 Miles 7 Lakes, 3 Rivers, 3 Creeks, 21 Portages
Difficulty: Rugged
Fisher map: 112

Introduction: This interesting loop will lead you through tiny creeks, small lakes, three rivers and a portion of the largest lake in the BWCA. From the public landing on Nels Lake, you will paddle east through Picket to Mudro and north to Fourtown Lake. Continuing east, you will cross Horse Lake and glide down the Horse River to the Basswood River on the Canadian border. Going up this beautiful river, you will view three scenic waterfalls before crossing a 330-rod portage into enormous Basswood Lake. Turning southwest, you will paddle through Jackfish Bay and into the Range River, through Sandpit Lake and back into the chain of lakes connecting Fourtown with Nels Lake.

Portages are evenly spaced throughout this route, the longest marking the midpoint of the loop. Three full days are required for the "average group"; four days would be more pleasant, but no doubt some rugged voyagers could do it in two. If the wind is strong out of the south or west, you may wish to reverse the route to avoid getting wind-bound on Jackfish Bay. If so, you will be entering the Boundary Waters via the Range River entry point (#23).

Anglers will find walleye inhabiting most of the lakes along this route. Northern pike and bluegill are also present in Fourtown and Horse lakes. You'll find lake trout, walleye, northern pike, bass and whitefish occupying the depths of Basswood Lake.

DAY 1: **Nels Lake,** p. 185 rods, **Picket Creek,** p. 30 rods, **Picket Lake,** p. 30 rods, **Mudro Creek, Mudro Lake,** p. 30 rods, **Fourtown Creek,** p. 110 rods, **Fourtown Creek,** p. 10 rods, **Fourtown Lake,** p. 1-3 rods, **Fourtown Lake,** p. 10 rods, **pond,** p. 70 rods, **Horse Lake.** Your first portage is well over ½ mile, but mostly level. A log bridge midway through the carry is slippery when wet, so watch your step. In periods of low water, the creeks between Nels and Fourtown Lake may be too dry to transport a loaded canoe. If so, you may be walking much of the day. On the other hand, if the water level is high, you may find it unnecessary to portage between Picket and Mudro; simply paddle under Forest Route 457 and through the narrow, shallow creek beyond. Several nice campsites are located on Horse Lake, which is much quieter than Fourtown.

DAY 2: **Horse Lake, rapids, Horse River, rapids, river,** p. 50 rods, **river, rapids, river,** p. 50 rods, **river,** p. 70 rods, **river, Basswood River,** p. 18 rods, **river,** p. 32 rods, **river,** p. 330 rods, **Basswood Lake.** This day is full of strenuous activity and beautiful scenery. In addition to the three sets of rapids on the Horse River around which portages are necessary, you will encounter at least three small rapids through which you can shoot, line or walk your canoe, depending on the water level and your ambition. Take time to contemplate the splendor of Lower Basswood Falls, Wheelbarrow Falls and Basswood Falls. That portion of the Basswood River in the vicinity of Basswood Falls is considered "dangerous waters". The safest route, therefore, is the 330-rod portage around it. If you prefer, however, you may take shorter portages instead. Use your own discetion, based on the water conditions and your own skill. Numerous good campsites are located in the narrows between Jackfish Bay and the main body of Basswood Lake.

DAY 3: **Jackfish Bay, Range River,** p. 20 rods, **river,** p. 40 rods, **Sandpit Lake,** p. 80 rods, **Mudro Lake, Mudro Creek,** p. 30 rods, **Picket Lake,** p. 30 rods, **Picket Creek,** p. 185 rods, **Nels Lake.** The 80-rod portage between Sandpit and Mudro Lakes looks innocent on the map; but it is not. The trail climbs steeply to 90 feet above Sandpit Lake before descending above 47 feet to Mudro Lake.

Route #22: The Crooked Border Route

7 Days, 78 Miles, 19 Lakes, 3 Rivers, 2 Creeks, 32 Portages
Difficulty: Challenging
Fisher maps: 107, 108, 112

Introduction: The Crooked Border route will take you through a well-balanced variety of small rivers and creeks, large lakes and small ones. From Fourtown Lake you'll paddle west and north through the chain of lakes leading to the Beartrap River and then down the river itself to Iron Lake. A side trip from Iron Lake will take you further northwest to the beautiful southeast end of Lac La Croix, where you may view old Indian pictographs and climb the legendary Warrior Hill. Turning east now, you'll have an opportunity to visit two of the spectacular falls bordering Iron Lake — Curtain and Rebecca — before challenging long and winding Crooked Lake. You will continue along the international border southeast up the Basswood River to splendid Lower Basswood Falls. From there you'll leave the historic Voyageurs' Highway and paddle southwest up the Horse River to Horse Lake and the chain of lakes that lead you back to your origin at Nels Lake.

Fishing is fairly good along this route. Walleye and/or northern pike, in particular, may be found in Nels, Mudro, Fourtown, Iron, Crooked and Horse lakes. Bluegill are abundant in Tin Can, Horse and Fourtown lakes.

Without the side trip to Lac La Croix, this scenic trip could easily be completed in six days by the average group of canoeists. But it would be a shame to be so close to the beauty of Lac La Croix without seeing it for yourself. Nearly one third of your time will be spent on small rivers and creeks, and there you should have ample opportunity to see various forms of wildlife. Although the international border lakes and the immediate vicinity of Fourtown Lake may be well-traveled, you should feel a degree of isolation throughout much of the rest of the route. Four beautiful waterfalls, numerous rapids and a host of attractive lakes all add up to a most delightful trip.

DAY 1: **Nels Lake,** p. 185 rods, **Picket Creek,** p. 30 rods, **Picket Lake,** p. 30 rods, **Mudro Creek, Mudro Lake,** p. 30 rods, **Fourtown Creek,** p. 110 rods, **creek,** p. 10 rods, **Fourtown Lake.** (See Comments for Day 1, Route #21.)

DAY 2: **Fourtown Lake,** p. 35 rods, **Boot Lake,** p. 15 rods, **Fairy Lake,** p. 50 rods, **Gun Lake,** p. 30 rods, **Gull Lake,** p. 35 rods, **Mudhole Lake,** p. 55 rods, **Thunder Lake.** Beyond Fourtown Lake, motors are prohibited, and travel here is relatively light. You'll encounter no difficulty on the portages, most of them being nearly level or downhill. The only significant climb is along the 30-rod trail from Gun to Gull Lake, which gains 24 feet.

DAY 3: **Thunder Lake,** p. 9 rods, **Beartrap Lake,** p. 200 rods, **Beartrap River,** p. 160 rods, **river, Sunday Lake,** p. 8 rods, **Beartrap River,** p. 10 rods, **river,** p. 35 rods, **river,** p. 110 rods, **Iron Lake.** You will be traveling downstream this day. Although two big portages present themselves, both are predominantly downhill. In fact, you will descend nearly 100 feet in all between Beartrap and Sunday lakes, and a total of 141 feet for the entire day. There are nine Forest Service campsites on Iron Lake. Find a good one and plan to stay for two nights.

DAY 4: **Iron Lake, Bottle Lake,** p. 80 rods, **Lac La Croix,** p. 80 rods, **Bottle Lake, Iron Lake.** Leave your tents and gear on Iron Lake this morning. Pack your lunch, first-aid kit, rain coat and camera, and paddle northwest for a pleasant outing on beautiful Lac La Croix. (See comments for Day 4,

Route #6.) Before returning to your campsite on Iron Lake, take time to paddle to Rebecca Falls at the outlet into McAree Lake. (See comments for Day 5, Route #6.) Don't forget to hang up your food pack in camp while you take this side trip. Blueberries are good, but you probably don't want to survive on them for the next three days.

DAY 5: **Iron Lake,** p. 120 rods, **Crooked Lake.** A beautiful 29-foot drop in the water level between Iron and Crooked lakes is called Curtain Falls. Take time to enjoy it. Your portage (US side) will be uphill, but not difficult. You may put in at any of three locations at the top of the falls: at the very brink of the falls, or about 100 feet farther into Crooked Lake, or yet another 100 feet or so east. The choice is yours, but I prefer the second during normal water conditions as the safest for a group that may not be strong enough to fight the swift current at the top of the falls. Use your own judgement and be careful. Many good campsites are scattered throughout Crooked Lake, including one at historic Table Rock, where many a Voyageur rested en route from Lake Superior to Lake Athabasca. An eagle's nest is located on an island near the east end of this long lake. A compass may be useful this day, as portions of Crooked Lake can be confusing even to an experienced guide.

DAY 6: **Crooked Lake, Basswood River,** p. 12 rods, **Basswood River, Horse River,** p. 70 rods, **river,** p. 50 rods, **river, rapids, river,** p. 50 rods, **river, rapids, river, rapids, Horse Lake,** p. 90 rods, **Tin Can Lake.** Lower Basswood Falls is a scenic 12-foot drop around which the first 12-rod portage passes. Although this route takes you up the Horse River, the mouth of which is just beyond this falls, you may wish to paddle beyond this confluence to another scenic cascade first — Wheelbarrow Falls, about ¾ mile up the Basswood River. While traveling up the Horse River, you will encounter at least three short, shallow rapids up which you will have to pull your canoe. These are located near the source of this pretty little river. A very nice campsite on Tin Can Lake is at the northwest corner of the lake, with ample space for more tents than you need. If time permits, cast your line for some of the many pan fish that inhabit the depths of this scenic lake.

DAY 7: **Tin Can Lake,** p. 160 rods, **Sandpit Lake,** p. 80 rods, **Mudro Lake, Mudro Creek,** p. 30 rods, **Picket Lake,** p. 30 rods, **Picket Creek,** p. 185 rods, **Nels Lake.** The two longest portages look threatening on the map (160 r. and 185 r.) but they are virtually level and not difficult.

Entry Point 22—Horse Lake

Permits: 244
Popularity Rank: 35
Daily Quota: 2

Location: Horse Lake is accessible from either Nels Lake (Route #23) or Fenske Lake (Route #24) located about straight north of Ely, 9 miles and 7 miles respectively. To get to Nels Lake, follow County Road 116 (the Echo Trail) north and west from County Road 88 for 10 miles, ¾ mile past the intersection with County Road 644 (North Arm Road). As the Echo Trail bends to the left, a one-lane primitive road branches to the right (east). Follow this narrow, winding path for ¾ mile to Nels Lake, where a small parking lot is adjacent to the public landing.

Description: Fenske Lake is also just off the Echo Trail, but only eight miles from its beginning at County Road 88. You'll see the lake on the right side of the road, one-tenth mile past the Fenske Lake Campground, which is an excellent spot to spend the night before your trip departure, whether it be via Route #23 or Route #24.

Since Horse Lake is several lakes and streams away from the Echo Trail, you will spend nearly all the first day for either route outside of the BWCA. But you will probably see more canoeists on (and after) Horse Lake than between the Echo Trail and Horse Lake, because neighboring Fourtown Lake is a popular "fly in" point of departure for fishermen and canoeists who want to get a head start on others who must drive the crooked Echo Trail. Although Horse Lake ranks only 35th in popularity as an entry point into the BWCA, don't be surprised by all the traffic that enters from the Fourtown Lake entry point.

Since these are designated as two separate entry points, if you find the Horse Lake entry point "closed" on the day when your trip is scheduled, you can take virtually the same route by entering the Boundary Waters through #21 (Fourtown) instead. Or you can alter your route a bit more, and enter the BWCA through the Range River entry point (#23). This is a good thing to remember, because I have frequently found at least one of these three entry points closed on the day of my scheduled departure. See #21-Fourtown Lake for other route ideas in this vicinity.

Route #23: The Crooked-Fairy Loop

4 Days, 50 Miles, 15 Lakes, 2 Rivers, 5 Creeks, 23 Portages
Difficulty: Challenging
Fisher maps: 108, 112

Introduction: This route will take you northeast from Nels Lake, through the chain of lakes to Horse Lake and down the Horse River to the Canadian border. Here you will pause to view two beautiful waterfalls, a unique display of Indian pictographs and a legendary campsite long ago used by the French-Canadian Voyageurs en route from Lake Superior to the northwestern hinterlands. Down the Basswood River, you'll follow the international border north and west into Crooked Lake. From Friday Bay you'll turn south and paddle through the small lakes and streams leading to Gun Lake. Going southeast through Fairy and Boot lakes, you will leave the BWCA via Fourtown Lake and return to Nels Lake by way of the chain of lakes and streams on which you spent your first day.

When completed, this route will have led you through some fairly heavily traveled parts of the Boundary Waters, as well as through some relatively little used parts. You will have experienced tiny creeks and larger rivers, small lakes and big ones, waterfalls and rapids, historic sites and wildlife — all within four days.

Bluegill, walleye and northern pike are prevalent throughout much of this loop, including in the lakes on which you will be camping.

When the water level is quite low, Picket Creek may present an immediate obstacle. At these times it can be unnavigable by a loaded canoe, and you'll find yourself walking much of the first and last days. During normal water conditions, however, there should be no problem, and during high water, you may even eliminate a couple portages!

DAY 1: **Nels Lake,** p. 185 rods, **Picket Creek,** p. 30 rods, **Picket Lake,** p. 30 rods, **Mudro Creek, Mudro Lake,** p. 80 rods, **Sandpit Lake,** p. 160 rods, **Tin Can Lake,** p. 90 rods, **Horse Lake.** Watch your step on that first long portage when crossing a log bridge midway through the carry. It is slippery when wet. When the water level is high, you may find it unnecessary to portage between Picket and Mudro lakes; simply paddle under Forest Route 457 and through the narrow, shallow creek beyond. Several nice campsites are located on Horse Lake. Don't be surprised to awaken the next morning to the awful roar of engines from sea planes depositing fishermen on nearby Fourtown Lake.

DAY 2: **Horse Lake, Horse River Rapids, river, rapids, river,** p. 50 rods, **river, rapids, river,** p. 50 rods, **river,** p. 70 rods, **river, Basswood River,** p. 12 rods, **Basswood River, Crooked Lake.** In addition to the three sets of rapids on the Horse River around which portages are necessary, you will encounter at least three small rapids through which you can shoot, line or walk your canoe, depending on the water level and your ambition. Right after the confluence of the Horse River with the Basswood River is Lower Basswood Falls. In addition, take time to paddle out of your way to Wheelbarrow Falls, ¾ mile up the Basswood River. Both are good targets for the canoeist with a photographic inclination. About a mile below Lower Basswood Falls on the US side of the river, you'll find several interesting figures painted on the granite cliffs. These are among the few bits of tangible evidence of the Indian civilization that once flourished in this region. Yet farther down the Basswood River, near the entrance to Wednesday Bay of Crooked Lake, is a reminder of another phase of our continent's history, Table Rock, a popular campsite for early French-Canadian Voyageurs. You will find several good campsites scattered throughout the American side of Crooked Lake. Keep your compass handy, as this long and winding lake can be confusing to even the experienced canoe-country camper.

DAY 3: **Crooked Lake, Friday Bay,** p. 95 rods, **Pappoose Creek, Pappoose Lake, creek,** p. 5 rods, **creek, Chippewa Lake, creek, Niki Lake,** p. 45 rods, **Wagosh Lake,** p. 300 rods, **Gun Lake.** (See comments of Day 5, Route #16.)

DAY 4: **Gun Lake,** p. 50 rods, **Fairy Lake,** p. 15 rods, **Boot Lake,** p. 35 rods, **Fourtown Lake,** p. 10 rods, **Fourtown Creek,** p. 110 rods, **creek,** p. 30 rods, **Mudro Lake, Mudro Creek,** p. 30 rods, **Picket Lake,** p. 30 rods, **Picket Creek,** p. 185 rods, **Nels Lake.** As on the first day, if the water level is high enough, you may be able to eliminate the 30-rod portage between Mudro and Picket lakes by paddling through the shallow stream between. Motors may be seen and heard along the route from Fourtown to Nels Lake, and you might even see a little four-wheel-drive traffic along Forest Route 457, at the portage between Mudro Creek and Picket Lake.

Route #24: The Canadian Border Route

9 Days, 114 Miles, 24 Lakes, 7 Rivers, 1 Creek, 41 Portages
Difficulty: Challenging
Fisher maps: 107, 108, 111, 112

Introduction: This route will take you north from Fenske Lake through a chain of beautiful small lakes and streams to Horse Lake. After paddling down the Horse River to the Basswood River at lovely Lower Basswood Falls, you will then head north and west along the international border, through the entire length of Lac La Croix to Loon Lake. Here you will depart from the land of the maple leaf and paddle south into the Pauness Lakes and up into the winding wilderness of the Little Indian Sioux River to its source at Otter Lake. From Cummings Lake you will turn south, leave the Boundary Waters at Crab Lake, and go into ever-popular and populated Burntside Lake. After crossing most of this beautiful, island-studded lake you will turn northeast again through the Dead River and into Twin, Everett and Fenske lakes.

This challenging route will require nine full, strenuous days for the average group of canoeists, without a layover day. Strong winds, however, could slow travel considerably on parts of Burntside Lake, the Little Indian Sioux River, Lac La Croix and Crooked Lake. The Little Indian Sioux River offers a fine opportunity to view moose, deer, beaver and other forms of wildlife, for it flows through a region in the BWCA seldom visited by tourists. Early summer is usually the best time to make this journey, since the Sioux and Range rivers may be too dry for navigation later in the summer, or during an especially dry year. Although there are numerous portages along the route, few are longer than 100 rods. Most of the route is well traveled, with the exception of the Sioux River south of the Echo Trail, where portage trails may be difficult to follow. In addition to the abundant wildlife and generally good fishing, voyagers will also find two good displays of prehistoric Indian pictographs adorning the sheer granite cliffs of Lac La Croix and the Basswood River. Splendid waterfalls, treacherous rapids, beautiful big lakes and quaint little ones all interconnect to create a fascinating variety of canoeing terrain.

DAY 1: **Fenske Lake,** p. 10 rods, **Little Sletten Lake,** p. 70 rods, **Sletten Lake,** p. 120 rods, **Tee Lake,** p. 48 rods, **Grassy Lake, beaver pond,** p. 24 rods, **Grassy River, Range River,** p. 1 rod, **river,** p. 30 rods, **river,** p. 10 rods, **river, Range Lake,** p. 340 rods, **Tin Can Lake.** Your first day will not take you into the BWCA. Nevertheless although a resort and several private cabins are situated at the west end of Fenske Lake, it won't take you long on this route to feel the essence of true wilderness. In fact, I rate this first day as one of the most interesting first days of any route in the BWCA. Of the five portages that greet you immediately, all but one are downhill. The only one to watch out for is the 70-rod trek between Little Sletten and Sletten lakes, which rather steeply crosses over the hill between. There may be a beaver dam between Grassy Lake and the pond thereafter, as well as on the upper part of the Grassy River and the lower stretches of the slow, winding, marshy Range River, near Range Lake. You will have two options for reaching Tin Can Lake from Range Lake. If portaging doesn't get you down, you can walk the entire distance, skirting Sandpit Lake along its east shore. Or you can portage 160 rods from Range to Sandpit, and another 160 rods from Sandpit to Tin Can (see detailed sketch of Range River region in Route #8). You will find a nice campsite near the north end of Tin Can Lake, with ample space for a large group.

DAY 2: **Tin Can Lake,** p. 90 rods, **Horse Lake, Horse River, rapids, river, rapids, river,** p. 50 rods, **river, rapids, river,** p. 50 rods, **river,** p. 70 rods, **river, Basswood River,** p. 12 rods, **Basswood River, Crooked Lake.** A short side trip to the Basswood River from its confluence with the Horse River will take you to scenic Wheelbarrow Falls. About ¾ mile downstream is Lower Basswood Falls, the last significant drop (12 feet) in the Basswood River before it enters Crooked Lake. Along the Horse River you will encounter at least three short, shallow rapids near the source, in addition to those farther down that require portaging. You should be able to shoot, line or walk your canoe through these, depending on the water level. A display of Indian paintings can be seen along the west shore of the Basswood River, about a mile downstream from Lower Basswood Falls. Several nice campsites are located between Lower Basswood Falls and Wednesday Bay of Crooked Lake, including Table Rock, long ago used by Voyageurs carrying furs from the Northwest to outposts on Lake Superior.

DAY 3: **Crooked Lake,** p. 120 rods, **Iron Lake.** There are many confusing bays, islands and peninsulas in Crooked Lake. (The eastern stretch may be confusing to even the most experienced Northwoods canoeist.) At least one eagle's nest is located near the east end, and it is not unusual to see eagles soaring overhead. Curtain Falls, with a total drop of 29 feet, separates Crooked and Iron lakes. Use caution and stay close to the left shoreline as you approach the misty brink of this beautiful falls. You'll see at least three possible portage landings on the US shoreline, ranging from a couple hundred feet away from the falls to the very edge. It appears from the portage trails that a good many people prefer the second possible landing, several rods from the falls' edge. Use your best judgement. Several campsites are within a mile of Curtain Falls on Iron Lake.

DAY 4: **Iron Lake, Bottle Lake,** p. 80 rods, **Lac La Croix.** Before leaving Iron Lake, take time to visit Rebecca Falls, at the outlet into McAree Lake. (See comments for Day 5, Route #6.)

Two points of historical interest await you on Lac La Croix: Warrior Hill and Indian pictographs. (See comments for Day 6, Route #10.) There are several outstanding campsites in the vicinity of the pictographs. Find one early, as this part of the border is usually heavily traveled by motor boats and canoeists alike. The beauty of this area makes the buzz of motors tolerable.

DAY 5: **Lac La Croix.** No portages today! Just a lot of paddling across the expanse of this 25-mile-long, potentially confusing lake. An Indian village is located at the source of the Namakan River, in the Neguaguon Lake Indian Reservation, adjacent to Quetico Provincial Park. Farther west along the Canadian shoreline are two resorts to break the monotony of paddling and to allow replenishment of any needed provisions.

DAY 6: **Lac La Croix,** p. 50 rods, **Loon Lake,** p. 160 rods, **Lower Pauness Lake,** p. 8 rods, **Upper Pauness Lake.** Don't miss the third set of Indian pictographs along the American shore just north of the 50-rod portage into Loon Lake. And take time during your steep uphill 160-rod climb to view the scenic granite gorge through which Devil's Cascade plunges 75 feet from Lower Pauness Lake to Loon Lake. Upper Pauness Lake is on a heavily used motor route, so grab a campsite as early as possible.

DAY 7: **Upper Pauness Lake, Little Indian Sioux River,** p. 60 rods, **river,** p. 120 rods, **river,** p. 8 rods, **river,** p. 120 rods, **river, Little Pony River,** p. 60 rods, **river,** p. 60 rods, **Bootleg Lake.** Watch out for traffic as you cross the Echo Trail at the 120-rod portage. From that point on, the number of canoes you see will greatly decrease, as motors are prohibited south of the Echo Trail. Campsites are few and far between on the swampy, winding Little Indian Sioux River. In fact, you will find no designated Forest Service campsites,

unless you divert your route up the Little Pony River to Bootleg Lake.

DAY 8: **Bootleg Lake,** p. 200 rods, **Little Indian Sioux
River,** p. 40 rods, **river,** p. 35 rods, **river,** p. 20 rods, **river,** p.
30 rods, **river,** p. 40 rods, **river,** p. 20 rods, **river,** p. 28 rods,
river, p. 120 rods, **Otter Lake,** p. 5 rods, **Cummings Lake.**
The nine short portages and considerable meandering make
travel deceivingly slow this day, as the Sioux becomes nar-
rower and shallower. Between portages it is virtually impossible to know EXACTLY where you are. Use the portages
as landmarks, and alert yourself to the GENERAL direction of
travel. Moose and deer are not uncommon sights along the
river.

DAY 9: **Cummings Lake,** p. 35 rods, **Korb Creek, Korb
Lake, Korb Creek,** p. 1-3 rods, **creek, Little Crab Lake,** p.
20 rods, **Crab Lake,** p. 320 rods, **Burntside Lake, Dead
River, East Twin Lake,** p. 14 rods, **Everett Lake,** p. 120
rods, **Fenske Lake.** You will encounter the longest portage of
the route this day, but it is a gently sloping downhill trek with
11 canoe rests evenly spread along a wide, smooth path.
Burntside Lake, with well over 100 picturesque islands, could
be confusing to even an experienced map reader. Keep constant count of the islands and bays as you weave through them
to the outlet into Twin Lakes. You'll see many cabins and
motor boats on popular Burntside Lake. If you wish to avoid
the last 140-rod portage into Fenske Lake, you can simply
walk along the Echo Trail (left) to your vehicle parked at the
access to Fenske Lake, less than a mile from the Everett Lake
portage.

Entry Point 23: Range River

Permits: 1312
Popularity Rank: 8
Daily Quota: 3

Location: The Range River is accessible to canoeists from Nels Lake, located almost 9 miles straight north of Ely. To get there, follow County Road 116 (the Echo Trail) north and west from County Road 88 for 10 miles, ¾ mile past the intersection with County Road 644 on the left. As the Echo Trail bends to the left, a one-lane primitive road branches to the right (east). Follow this narrow, winding path for ¾ mile to Nels Lake, where a small parking lot is adjacent to the public landing.

Description: Camping is prohibited at the landing, but a Forest Service campsite is located nearby on the lake, with a path leading north to it from the landing. If this is occupied or inconvenient, you may wish to spend the night before your trip at Fenske Lake Campground, two miles closer to Ely on the Echo Trail.

The four lakes leading to the Range River and the river itself are outside the Boundary Waters. Motors are allowed through the entry point, and a resort is strategically located just west of the BWCA. Consequently, most visitor use permits are granted to operators of motorboats, only 10 percent being issued to parties using canoes without motors. Furthermore, mighty Basswood Lake is also open to motorized craft. So neither of the routes suggested through this entry point is recommended to those in search of a pristine wilderness expedition. Probably the quietest part of the two trips, in fact, is the part outside the BWCA, between the Echo Trail and Jackfish Bay.

Route #25: The Basswood Bays Loop

5 Days, 48 Miles, 5 Lakes, 1 River, 2 Creeks, 13 Portages
Difficulty: Easy
Fisher map: 112

Introduction: This little loop will take you east from the Nels Lake landing, through a chain of small lakes and shallow creeks, to the Range River. Continuing east, you will soon enter into another world of canoeing on enormous Basswood Lake. Here you will first paddle northeast through Jackfish Bay and into the main part of Basswood. From U.S. Point, then, you will turn south and paddle past Canada Customs at

Ottawa Island, before angling off to the southwest toward Hoist Bay. From Hoist Bay, you will paddle northward into Back Bay. A short portage into Pipestone Bay will give your legs the stretching they need. Then you will paddle north and west to Jackfish Bay again and follow it southwest to the Range River. From here on, you will be backtracking through the lakes and streams that brought you here from Nels Lake three days earlier.

Nowhere on this route will you be safe from the sound of motors, although most of the motor traffic will be encountered inside the Boundary Waters. Besides the wakes from motor-boats, gail-force winds are also an ever-present threat on big Basswood Lake. If strong winds are forecast, you would be wise to avoid this route. And if a storm suddenly threatens, get off the lake immediately!

Low water level may also be a problem in the creeks leading from Nels Lake to Basswood. There are periods in late August — even earlier in an especially dry summer — when these creeks are too low to allow passage of a heavily loaded canoe.

For the anglers in your group, Basswood Lake contains walleye, northern pike, smallmouth bass, lake trout and whitefish. You will also find walleye in the lakes west of the Range River.

DAY 1: **Nels Lake,** p. 185 rods, **Picket Creek,** p. 30 rods, **Picket Lake,** p. 30 rods, **Mudro Creek, Mudro Lake,** p. 80 rods, **Sandpit Lake,** p. 40 rods, **Range River,** p. 20 rods, **river, Jackfish Bay.** Watch your step on the first portage: a log bridge crosses a creek midway through the carry, and it is slippery when wet. If the water level is high, you may find it unnecessary to portage between Picket and Mudro lakes. Simply paddle under Forest Route 457 and through the narrow, shallow creek beyond. The 80-rod portage from Mudro to Sandpit Lake is steep, but mostly downhill. You will find several campsites along the southeast shore of Jackfish Bay.

DAY 2: **Jackfish Bay, Basswood Lake.** For the sake of variety on this long day of paddling, you may wish to visit Basswood Falls at the outlet of the Basswood River from Basswood Lake. Plan to camp in the vicinity of U.S. Point, where the lake bends to the south.

DAY 3: **Basswood Lake, Hoist Bay, Back Bay.** You may wish to paddle past and take a picture of the Canadian Customs station located south of Ottawa Island. Compared to the rest of Basswood, you will find a degree of solitude in Back Bay.

DAY 4: **Back Bay,** p. 70 rods, **Pipestone Bay, Jackfish Bay, Range River,** p. 20 rods, **river,** p. 40 rods, **Sandpit Lake.** If the only campsite on Sandpit Lake is taken, you might like to portage an easy ½ mile north to Tin Can Lake, a pan-fisherman's paradise, where three campsites are located near the north end.

DAY 5: **Sandpit Lake,** p. 80 rods, **Mudro Lake, Mudro Creek,** p. 30 rods, **Picket Lake,** p. 30 rods, **Picket Creek,** p. 185 rods, **Nels Lake.** If you don't remember that 80-rod portage between Sandpit and Mudro lakes, you will after this day! Now it is uphill, climbing steeply to 90 feet above Sandpit Lake, before descending 27 feet to Mudro Lake.

Route #26: The Basswood-Snowbank Loop

8 Days, 76 Miles, 14 Lakes, 1 River, 2 Creeks, 22 Portages
Difficulty: Challenging
Fisher maps: 112, 113

Introduction: This route will take you through the busiest, most heavily traveled part of all the Boundary Waters Canoe Area. After your entry into the BWCA from the Range River, you will paddle eastward throughout the full length of enormous Basswood Lake. From Bayley Bay, you will continue southeast, past Canadian Customs, through Sucker Lake and into Ensign Lake. Turning south here, you will portage into Boot Lake and then into Snowbank Lake. From the west end of Snowbank, you will portage and paddle your way northwest through Moose and Wind lakes to the southernmost bay of mighty Basswood. Four bays farther on you will find yourself back at the Range River, and from there you will continue moving west through the smaller lakes and streams that lead back to the Echo Trail.

After your entry into the BWCA, don't expect to find solitude anywhere along this route. This region is served by the first and third most popular entry points, Moose and Fall lakes, as well as the eleventh, Snowbank Lake. All these, in addition to the Range River, offer motor routes to the Canadian border, and many of the motorists who use them head directly for Basswood Lake. Besides the extensive traffic along the route, resorts and private cabins will also be seen along the south shores of Snowbank and Moose lakes.

If this does not discourage you, strong winds may. High, treacherous waves caused by gail-force winds are not uncommon on much of Basswood Lake. Regardless of the direction of the wind, at least some portion of this mammoth lake will feel the effects. The same is true for big Snowbank Lake. Even if the lakes are calm when you start across them, be alert for threatening changes in the weather and stay close to the lee shoreline.

A major reason for the heavy traffic on these lakes is the fishing opportunity. You will find all the major North Woods species in Basswood Lake — lake trout, northern pike, walleye, smallmouth bass and whitefish. Walleye, northern pike and bass are also plentiful in Moose, Ensign and Snowbank lakes. Tiny Flash Lake is a good place to catch northern pike. Snowbank has long been a favorite haunt of anglers in search of the elusive lake trout, but it has recently shown signs of being "fished out."

DAY 1: **Nels Lake,** p. 185 rods, **Picket Creek,** p. 30 rods, **Picket Lake,** p. 30 rods, **Mudro Creek, Mudro Lake,** p. 80 rods, **Sandpit Lake,** p. 40 rods, **Range River,** p. 20 rods, **river, Jackfish Bay.** (See comments for Day 1, Route #25.)

DAY 2: **Jackfish Bay, Basswood Lake.** (See comments for Day 2, Route #25.)

DAY 3: **Basswood Lake, Bayley Bay,** p. 20 rods, **Sucker Lake, New Found Lake,** p. 35 rods, **Splash Lake, Ensign Lake.** You will pass a Canadian Customs station and a Ranger Cabin just south of Ottawa Island, where Basswood Lake bends east. You will portage past another Customs station at Prairie Portage, between Bayley Bay and Sucker Lake. A strong west wind can whip up dangerous waves between these points. A narrow, shallow rapids separates Splash Lake from Ensign Lake, but under normal conditions you should be able to paddle through it with no problem. Be sure to hang your food well above the ground this night, as bears are a common nuisance in this area.

DAY 4: **Ensign Lake,** p. 220 rods, **Boot Lake,** p. 30 rods, **pond,** p. 50 rods, **Snowbank Lake.** The southwest part of Snowbank is outside of the Boundary Waters, and four active resorts operate there. If you prefer a quieter location at which to spend the night, continue across a rocky 140-rod portage to Flash Lake. There are no Forest Service campsites here, but, since it is outside of the BWCA, you may choose a suitable spot to make your own. Flash Lake offers an oasis of solitude between two busy motor routes.

DAY 5: **Snowbank Lake,** p. 140 rods, **Flash Lake,** p. 350 rods, **Moose Lake,** p. 170 rods, **Wind Lake.** This will be your roughest day of the trip. The long portage from Flash to Moose Lake meets the Moose Lake Road after 250 rods, and

then follows this wide gravel road downhill for about 100 rods
to the busy public landing on Moose Lake. You will find the
first 250 rods to be a rather scenic trail, if you can take your
mind off the weight on your shoulders. The next portage path
climbs nearly 80 feet before dropping back down to Wind
Lake, where several good campsites may be found.

DAY 6: **Wind Lake,** p. 170 rods, **Wind Bay, Basswood
Lake, Hoist Bay, Back Bay,** p. 70 rods, **Pipestone Bay.** You
will see the north end of the busy 4-Mile Truck Portage at the
south end of Hoist Bay. Many of the large motorboats seen on
Basswood Lake come this way from Fall Lake.

DAY 7: **Pipestone Bay, Jackfish Bay, Range River,** p.
20 rods, **river,** p. 40 rods, **Sandpit Lake.** (See comments for
Day 4, Route #25.)

DAY 8: **Sandpit Lake,** p. 80 rods, **Mudro Lake, Mudro
Creek,** p. 30 rods, **Picket Lake,** p. 30 rods, **Picket Creek,** p.
185 rods, **Nels Lake.** (See comments for Day 5, Route #25.)

Ch. 4:

Entry from the Fernberg Road

The North-Central Region

The Fernberg Road is probably known by more visitors to the BWCA than any other highway. Three of the 10 most popular entry points are served by this road, including Moose Lake, the most heavily used entry point in all the BWCA. Three other entry points included in this guide are also served by the Fernberg Road.

To get there, simply follow State Highway 169 northeast from the Voyageur Visitor Center, past the small town of Winton, and across the Lake County line. This highway becomes the Fernberg Road, an extension of Highway 169 into Lake County.

The road surface is blacktop all the way to its end at the Lake One landing. Generally, it is a good road, with relatively few sharp curves. Locals who are familiar with the road drive it quite fast, so beware . . .

Entry Point 24—Fall Lake

Permits: 2992
Popularity Rank: 3
Daily Quota: 23

Location: Fall Lake is located about three miles north-east of Ely. Follow the Fernberg Road 5 miles from the Voyageur Visitor Center to Forest Route 551, the Fall Lake Road. Turn left and follow this good, paved road slightly more than 1 mile to the public access and parking lot on the left side of the road.

Description: Farther down the Fall Lake Road you will find a Forest Service campground, a good place to spend the night before your trip.

Fall Lake is by far the most convenient entry point into the Boundary Waters, being located so close to Ely and accessible by such good paved roads. At its northeast end is the 4-Mile Truck Portage, on which heavy motor boats are easily transported to popular Basswood Lake, on the international boundary. Along with several resorts and many private cabins, most local outfitters also have bases on this lake. Consequently, traffic into the BWCA is heavy, and only half of it is canoes without motors.

Although Fall Lake itself has little appeal, it does provide easy access into big, beautiful Basswood Lake, the enticing Basswood River, and a degree of wilderness solitude beyond. If you can tolerate the wakes of passing motor boats and the frustrating winds on Basswood, you'll surely find a worthwhile trip from a Fall Lake origin. See Entry Point 26-Wood Lake for other route ideas in this area.

Route #27: The Four Falls Route

4 Days, 46 Miles, 6 Lakes, 3 Rivers, 14 Portages
Difficulty: Challenging
Fisher map: 112

Introduction: This short loop will lead you north to the Canadian border, via Fall, Newton and Basswood lakes, and around Pipestone Falls. Then you will paddle down the beautiful Basswood River, where you will view three more attractive waterfalls. Turning south from Lower Basswood Falls, you will paddle up the tranquil Horse River to Horse Lake before returning to Basswood Lake via the Range River. Then you will backtrack through familiar waters as you return south to your origin at Fall Lake.

If the wind is strong, you should probably consider another entry point that does not lead to Basswood Lake, which is both frustrating and dangerous at such times. In fact, if the weather is merely threatening, avoid wide open stretches on this lake. Similarly, beware of dangerous waters on the Basswood River, which has tempted and destroyed many a foolish voyager over the years.

Motors are permitted on much of this route. Between Basswood Falls and the Range River, however, you will find the going much quieter than elsewhere. You will surely find the Basswood and Horse Rivers rewarding. But you may find the paddling to be tedious on the first and last days of this challening route.

Northern pike and walleye inhabit much of the water along this route. You will also find smallmouth bass and lake trout in Basswood Lake, and bluegill in Horse and Tin Can lakes. I have found parts of the lower Basswood River, in particular, to be tastily rewarding.

DAY 1: **Fall Lake,** p. 80 rods, **Newton Lake,** p. 40 rods, **Pipestone Bay of Basswood Lake.** Again, beware of wind and the wakes of motor boats. Campsites are plentiful at the north end of Pipestone Bay.

DAY 2: **Jackfish Bay, Basswood Lake,** p. 330 rods, **Basswood River,** p. 32 rods, **river,** p. 18 rods, **river.** You will see three scenic waterfalls this day: Basswood Falls, Wheelbarrow Falls, and Lower Basswood Falls. That portion of the Basswood River near its source is considered "dangerous waters." The safest route, therefore, is the 330-rod portage around it that I recommend. If you prefer, however, you can take shorter portages instead. Use your own discretion, based on the water conditions and your own skill. If the campsites are not available (or suitable) between Wheelbarrow and Lower Basswood Falls, you may wish to portage an easy 12 rods around Lower Basswood Falls to Crooked Lake, on which several nice campsites are located near the base of the falls. You may wish to paddle another mile downstream to view a display of Indian rock paintings decorating the sheer granite cliffs along the west shoreline.

DAY 3: **Basswood River, Horse River,** p. 70 rods, **river,** p. 50 rods, **river, rapids, river,** p. 50 rods, **river, rapids, river, rapids, Horse Lake,** p. 90 rods, **Tin Can Lake,** p. 160 rods, **Sandpit Lake,** p. 40 rods, **Range River,** p. 20 rods, **river, Jackfish Bay of Basswood Lake.** In addition to the three sets of rapids on the Horse River around which portages are necessary, you will encounter at least three small rapids up which you will have to pull your canoe. (See detailed sketch of the Range River region in Route #8.)

DAY 4: **Jackfish Bay, Pipestone Bay,** p. 40 rods, **Newton Lake,** p. 80 rods, **Fall Lake.** If wind discourages paddling on Jackfish Bay, you may wish to take a short-cut by portaging 60 rods into a small bay between Jackfish and Pipestone Bays.

Route #28: The Basswood Lake Loop

5 Days, 62 Miles, 7 Lakes, 8 Portages

Difficulty: Easy

Fisher maps: 112, 113

Introduction: This heavily traveled route will take you north from Fall Lake to the international boundary, via Newton and Basswood lakes. You will follow enormous Basswood Lake east along the Canadian border to Sucker Lake, where you will turn southwest and follow the busy Moose Chain to the south edge of the BWCA on Moose Lake. You'll then cross back to Basswood Lake through Wind Lake, and follow the southern bays of this mighty lake back to your origin at Fall Lake.

At trip's end you will have crossed only eight portages, only two of which are challenging. The vast majority of your time will be spent paddling across the largest lake in the BWCA, Basswood, where motor traffic is heavy and strong winds a constant threat. As mentioned for Route #27, if menacing winds prevail, consider a different route through a different entry point. Basswood Lake is not a good place to be in the middle of a gale.

Throughout most of the route you will find smallmouth bass, northern pike and walleye beneath you. Lake trout are also present in Basswood Lake. Since motors are permitted throughout the route, you will see many fishermen everywhere.

DAY 1: **Fall Lake,** p. 80 rods, **Newton Lake,** p. 40 rods, **Pipestone Bay of Basswood Lake.** (See comments for Day 1, Route #27.)

DAY 2: **Pipestone Bay, Jackfish Bay, Basswood Lake, Bayley Bay.** You may wish to visit Canadian Customs just south of Ottawa Island. You won't find a trading post there, and the officer there is too busy to be bothered, but the whole setting will surely warrant a photograph. Again, beware of wind and the wakes of motor boats throughout Basswood Lake.

DAY 3: **Bayley Bay,** p. 20 rods, **Sucker Lake, New Found Lake, Moose Lake,** p. 170 rods, **Wind Lake.** This last portage into Wind Lake is, no doubt, the most challenging trek on this route, climbing nearly 80 feet and extending over ½ mile. Because of it, however, Wind Lake is a little more peaceful then the rest of the route. Several campsites are available around the lake.

DAY 4: **Wind Lake,** p. 170 rods, **Wind Bay, Basswood Lake, Hoist Bay, Back Bay,** p. 70 rods, **Pipestone Bay.** The half-mile path leading out of Wind Lake is downhill, and not as difficult as the one leading into the lake at the other end.

DAY 5: **Pipestone Bay,** p. 40 rods, **Newton Lake,** p. 80 rods, **Fall Lake.** This will be the reverse of your first day. Portages are still not difficult, but uphill this time.

Entry Point 25 — Moose Lake

Permits: 7705
Popularity Rank: 1
Daily Quota: 32

Location: Moose Lake is located 16 miles northeast of Ely, a scant 4 miles south of the Canadian border. To get there, follow the Fernberg Road 16 miles from the Voyageurs Visitor Center to Forest Foute 438 (Moose Lake Road). Turn left and follow the gravel road north for nearly 3 miles to the Public Landing.

Description: A good public campground is at Fall Lake, just off the Fernberg Road, about 14 miles toward Ely. This offers a good place to spend the night prior to your canoe trip.

Moose Lake is by far the busiest of all entry points into the Boundary Waters Canoe Area. On more than one occasion I have passed well over 100 canoes on the Moose chain of lakes, and that includes neither those paddling in my direction nor the many motor boats used by fishermen in the area! Of the 7,705 permits issued in 1977, only 56% were issued to groups using canoes without motors. This was due in large part to the fact that the Moose chain is one of two major motor routes to the ever-popular Basswood Lake (the other is from Fall Lake). It is also the quickest link to Canada's Quetico Provincial Park.

Many resorts, outfitters and private cabins are located at the southwest end of the lake, and most of the once-good campsites on the chain are now closed due to overuse. The scenery is not especially attractive from Moose to the Canadian border, and signs of wildlife during the busy summer months are virtually nonexistent.

Nevertheless, if all of these facts do not drive you away, you will find that the busy Moose Chain does *lead* you to some of the most beautiful, interesting and peaceful lakes and streams in all the BWCA. Don't expect to experience total solitude anywhere on either of the routes suggested below between Memorial Day and Labor Day, but, if sharing "your" lakes with other nature lovers doesn't bother you, you'll surely find these routes delightful. See Entry Point 27-Snowbank Lake for other route ideas in this area.

Route #29: The Knife River-Disappointment Loop

4 Days, 34 Miles, 19 Lakes, 1 River, 18 Portages

Difficulty: Challenging

Fisher map: 113

Introduction: This short loop should probably be classified with two difficulty ratings: the first half EASY, and the last half RUGGED. Your first day should bring you to no more than one portage as you paddle your way northeast along the busy Moose chain of lakes to the Canadian border. Following the border farther northeast, you'll walk your canoe up the series of Knife River rapids to big Knife Lake. From Knife, you'll depart from the international boundary and turn back to the southwest through Vera, Ensign and a series of small lakes to island-studded Disappointment Lake. Then westward, you will slip through Parent Lake and across giant Snowbank Lake to Flash Lake and your origin at the Moose Lake public landing. The entire loop is along a motor route.

If the winds are westerly (as they usually are) you will make good time, but if they swoop down from the north, beware of Snowbank Lake! All along the route, campsites are at a premium, so don't wait too late each day to find yours. Throughout most of the loop, you'll find northern pike, walleye and bass inhabiting the depths, as well as lake trout in Knife and Snowbank lakes.

Although deer and moose are seldom seen along the route, the same is not true for bears, unfortunately. Be sure to tie your food pack up in the air at night, and during the day when you are away from camp. This is particularly important between the Knife River and Ensign Lake.

DAY 1: **Moose Lake, New Found Lake, Sucker Lake, Birch Lake.** This day is short for no other reason than the lack of available Forest Service campsites between Birch and Knife lakes. Although much of the traffic from Moose Lake heads east to Ensign Lake or northwest to Basswood Lake, a good deal of it continues along the border to Knife Lake. On a busy weekend and in August, it is not unusual to find all the "legal" campsites from Birch through the southwest end of Knife Lake taken. You have two alternatives: 1) stop early, or 2) stop at Canada customs for the necessary permits that will enable you to camp on the Canadian side of these busy lakes.

DAY 2: **Birch Lake,** p. 48 rods, **Carp Lake,** p. 16 rods, **Knife River,** p. 15 rods, **Seed Lake,** p. 15 rods, **Knife River,** p. 75 rods, **Knife Lake,** p. 200 rods, **Vera Lake.** If the water level is high enough (but not too high) you can eliminate all of the portages on the Knife River by walking your canoe up the series of gentle rapids around which the portages pass. Only on two occasions will you have to lift your canoe and gear — around a low falls and over a small dam. Be sure to visit Dorothy Molter's resort on a cluster of three small islands located straight east of the portage into Knife Lake. There you will find home-made root beer — ice cold — and an assortment of candy bars. And you will enjoy your visit with Dorothy, one of two fascinating people allowed to live within the BWCA.

The 200-rod portage from Knife to Vera Lake is a tough one, climbing steeply to an elevation of 80 feet above Knife. But, thanks to it, canoe traffic on Vera is much lighter than on either Knife or Ensign Lake. A nice campsite is found along the north shore soon after the portage.

DAY 3: **Vera Lake,** p. 180 rods, **Ensign Lake,** p. 53 rods, **Ashigan Lake,** p. 105 rods, **Gibson Lake,** p. 25 rods, **Cattyman Lake,** p. 10 rods, **Adventure Lake,** p. 40 rods, **Jitterbug Lake,** p. 15 rods, **Ahsub Lake,** p. 25 rods, **Disappointment Lake.** Very low water could cause some difficulty between Gibson and Ahsub lakes, and rocks and stumps may present a hazard at the northwest end of Cattyman Lake. Jitterbug, which is always shallow, may be too low for navigation near the portage into Ahsub Lake, requiring an extended portage through marshy terrain. You'll see a lot of daytime traffic (with Day Use Permits) on Disappointment Lake, coming from the four resorts on Snowbank Lake.

DAY 4: **Disappointment Lake,** p. 85 rods, **Parent Lake,** p. 80 rods, **Snowbank Lake,** p. 140 rods, **Flash Lake,** p. 250 rods to the **Moose Lake Road.** Numerous motor boats and wind are potential hazards on Snowbank Lake, a long-time favorite among fishermen in search of lake trout. Flash Lake is a delightfully peaceful change from Snowbank. Unfortunately, however, your trip must end with its longest portage — a nearly level trek from Flash Lake to the Moose Lake Road. You will find the parking lot a short distance down the road (turn right off the portage trail).

Route #30: The Silver Falls-Kekekabic Route

8 Days, 94 Miles, 31 Lakes, 1 River, 1 Creek, 37 Portages
Difficulty: Challenging
Fisher maps: 109, 113

Introduction: This popular route will take you northeast

along the Canadian border to mighty Saganaga Lake, less than three miles from the Gunflint Trail. You will spend two nights on this beautiful lake to accommodate a side trip to magnificent Silver Falls, northwest of Cache Bay. From Saganaga Lake, you will turn southwest and follow a lovely chain of lakes to impressive Kekekabic Lake. South to Fraser and Thomas Lakes, you will then turn northwest through Ima, Jordan and a group of tiny lakes to popular Ensign Lake. Finally, you will retrace your path through New Found and Moose lakes to the Public Landing.

Virtually every inch of this route is very popular in summertime, about three-fourths of it being designated for motors. Portages are neither long nor difficult, though some are rather steep, particularly between Kekekabic and Fraser lakes. Seldom if ever will you feel isolated, and at times you may even feel crowded. Nevertheless, the route offers many scenic attractions, and enticing opportunities for the avid angler. Lake trout inhabit the depths under much of the route, including Knife, Cypress, Saganaga, Alpine, Kekekabic and Thomas Lakes. Northern pike, walleye and bass are also found in most of these waters, as well as in the Moose chain of lakes and Red Rock, Fraser, Ima and Ensign lakes, among others.

If winds are out of the south or west, you should make excellent time traveling along the Canadian border to Saganaga Lake. The water level should make little difference to your plans, except as regards your ability to walk several rapids and thus to eliminate portages.

DAY 1: **Moose Lake, New Found Lake, Sucker Lake, Birch Lake.** (See comments for Day 1, Route #29.)

DAY 2: **Birch Lake,** p. 48 rods, **Carp Lake,** p. 16 rods, **Knife River,** p. 15 rods, **Seed Lake,** p. 15 rods, **Knife River,** p. 75 rods, **Knife Lake.** (See comments for Day 2, Route #29.) Although the southwest end of Knife Lake is often crowded with campers, vacant campsites should appear as you get closer to Little Knife Portage into Cypress Lake.

DAY 3: **Knife Lake,** p. 12 rods, **Cypress Lake,** p. 80 rods, **Swamp Lake,** p. 5 rods, **Saganaga Lake.** Cypress Lake (Ottertrack on some maps) is long, narrow and lined with high bluffs and a rocky shoreline. It is one of my favorites. Beside it you will see cabins belonging to Benny Ambrose, who (like Dorothy Molter on Knife Lake) resides permanently in the BWCA. Unlike Dorothy, however, Benny does not operate a concession stand, so please respect his right to privacy. Saganaga is a big, beautiful lake that is heavily traveled because of its easy access from the Gunflint Trail. Motor boats are permitted here. Several nice campsites are in the vicinity of American Point.

DAY 4: **Side trip through Cache Bay** to **Silver Falls.** Silver Falls are by far the highest and most spectacular falls in this guide. Although you do not need a permit from Canadian Customs to visit the falls, you will have to stop at the Canadian Ranger Station on the southernmost of the three islands near the entrance to Cache Bay to buy a travel permit into Quetico Provincial Park. The small fee and the extra paddling across gusty Cache Bay are well worth it. (Bears are reported in the area, so don't leave your food packs on the ground while you are away from camp.)

DAY 5: **Saganaga Lake, Red Rock Bay,** p. 10 rods, **Red Rock Lake,** p. 50 rods, **Alpine Lake,** p. 45 rods, **Jasper Lake,** p. 25 rods, **King Fisher Lake,** p. 38 rods, **Ogishkemuncie Lake.** You will be on a motor route during much of this day, but motors are not allowed beyond the portage into Jasper Lake. If the water level permits, you may wish to walk your canoe up the rapids between King Fisher and Ogishkemuncie lakes, and eliminate the 38-rod portage. Watch for eagles on Saganaga Lake: at least one nest is near-by. Along the southeast shore of Red Rock Bay you'll witness the charred remains of a 1976 fire that ravaged the area. Ogishkemuncie is a long and pretty lake, with many small islands and numerous good campsites. Because of its great popularity, you should look for a campsite early.

DAY 6: **Ogishkemuncie Lake,** p. 15 rods, **Annie Lake,** p. 15 rods, **Jean Lake,** p. 15 rods, **Eddy Lake,** five portages through **"Kekekabic Ponds," Kekekabic Lake,** p. 85 rods, **Strup Lake,** p. 10 rods, **Wisini Lake,** p. 90 rods, **Ahmakose Lake,** p. 30 rods, **Gerund Lake,** p. 15 rods, **Fraser Lake.** With 13 portages, this day should prove to be the toughest one of the trip. On the other hand, it is also your only full day on lakes where motors are prohibited. The first eight portages leading into Kekekabic Lake are short and easy, providing more of a nuisance than a challenge, and your entrance to Kekekabic makes it all worth while anyway. The narrow entrance to this magnificent lake gradually widens as it winds to the west and the high-rising bluffs that encircle it come into view. In the distance, you'll see hills rising as high as 400 feet above the lake. A trail from the south shore of the lake will take you to a fire-watch tower about a half-mile hike up from the shoreline, where you will find an incredible view of the surrounding terrain.

The next three portages provide some challenge. The 85-rod portage out of Kekekabic climbs more than 100 feet before descending 21 feet to Strup Lake. The next short portage ascends 17 feet in 10 rods. And, although Wisini and Ahmakose lakes lie at nearly the same elevation, the 90-rod path between them climbs 54 feet above their level.

DAY 7: **Fraser Lake, Thomas Lake,** p. 5 rods, **pond,** p. 10 rods, **creek,** p. 10 rods, **creek,** p. 10 rods, **Hatchet Lake,** p. 50 rods, **Ima Lake,** p. 5 rods, **Jordan Lake,** p. 55 rods, **Cattyman Lake,** p. 25 rods, **Gibson Lake,** p. 105 rods, **Ashigan Lake.** If the water level is high enough, you can walk, line or shoot your canoe down the narrow rapids around which two of the 10-rod portages pass between Thomas and Hatchet lakes. The first 10-rod portage crosses the famed Kekekabic Trail. A short hike off the 25-rod portage into Gibson Lake will lead you to a waterfall, where the water drops 37 feet from the stump-filled pond.

DAY 8: **Ashigan Lake,** p. 53 rods, **Ensign Lake, Splash Lake,** p. 35 rods, **New Found Lake, Moose Lake.** The last day is along a busy motor route. A shallow and narrow rapids separates Ensign and Splash lakes, but under normal water conditions you should be able to shoot through it easily.

Entry Point 26—Wood Lake

Permits: 79
Popularity Rank: 47
Daily Quota: 1

Location: The portage to Wood Lake is located on the north (left) side of the Fernberg Road, 12½ miles from the Voyageur Visitor Center, near a small parking lot. The campground at Fall Lake is a good place to spend the night before your trip, and the only public campground along the Fernberg Road. Follow the Fall Lake Road north from its junction with the Fernberg Road, 7½ miles closer to Ely.

Description: Most of Wood Lake lies outside of the Boundary Waters Canoe Area and is, therefore, a popular fishing lake for guests at nearby resorts. Nevertheless, motors are not permitted to enter the BWCA from Wood Lake. So the two lakes between Wood and Basswood lakes are rather peaceful and lightly traveled. This provides the wilderness canoeist with a much more pleasant access to Basswood Lake than does either the Moose Lake or Fall Lake entry route. The only draw-back is the initial half-mile-plus portage from the Fernberg Road. (See Entry Point 24-Fall Lake for other route ideas in this vicinity.)

Route #31: The Basswood Lake Loop

3 Days, 34 Miles, 4 Lakes, 1 Creek, 9 Portages
Difficulty: Easy
Fisher map: 112

Introduction: This easy loop takes you straight north from Wood Lake to the Canadian border on big Basswood Lake. You'll follow the international boundary north and west for several miles, before looping back to the south and east through portions of four of Basswood's bays. You will then backtrack through Good, Hula and Wood lakes to your origin at the Fernberg Road.

The only challenging part of this route is at the beginning and the end, where you encounter the same 196-rod portage. If winds are strong or the weather is ominous, you should probably avoid potentially dangerous Basswood Lake, where waves can quickly swell to a height of three feet or more.

The only lakes in this route on which motors are not allowed are Hula and Good. All of Basswood is open to motor boats, and it is extremely popular with fishermen. There you will find walleye, northern pike, smallmouth bass and lake trout.

DAY 1: P. 196 rods, **Wood Lake,** p. 72 rods, **Hula Lake,** p. 110 rods, **Good Lake,** p. 2 rods, **Good Creek, Hoist Bay, Basswood Lake.** You will have no trouble finding campsites on or in the vicinity of Washington Island. Be certain that you are camped in the US, unless you have obtained clearance from the Ottawa Island Customs to camp in Canada.

DAY 2: **Basswood Lake, Jackfish Bay, Pipestone Bay,** p. 70 rods, **Back Bay.** Beware the wakes from motor boats throughout this huge lake. High, treacherous waves caused by gail-force winds, too, are not uncommon on Basswood Lake. Regardless of the direction of the wind, at least some portion of the lake will feel the effects. Even if the lake is calm when you start across, be alert for threatening changes in the weather and stay close to the lee shoreline. For the sake of variety on this long day of paddling, you may wish to visit two places of special interest. Even though you won't be going into Canada, you'll surely find the customs station south of Ottawa Island worthy of a photograph. Basswood Falls, at the outlet of the Basswood River from the northwest corner of Basswood Lake, also deserves a photograph.

Compared to the rest of Basswood Lake, you may find a degree of solitude in Back Bay.

DAY 3: **Back Bay, Hoist Bay, Good Creek,** p. 2 rods, **Good Lake,** p. 110 rods, **Hula Lake,** p. 72 rods, **Wood Lake,** p. 196 rods. You will see civilization at the south end of Hoist Bay, which is the northeast end of the busy 4-Mile Truck Portage from Fall Lake. Many of the large motorboats seen on Basswood Lake come this way. The entrance to Good Creek is just east of there. From that point on, you will be retracing the path of your first day.

Route #32: The Triangle Loop

4 Days, 48 Miles, 13 Lakes, 1 Creek, 15 Portages
Difficulty: Challenging
Fisher maps: 112, 113

Introduction: This not-too-difficult route will take you north to Basswood Lake, and then east along the Canadian border to Birch Lake. From the east end of Birch you will portage into two seldom-visited lakes before entering Ensign Lake and turning your course back west. From Moose Lake you will portage into Wind Lake and then into Basswood

Lake, where you begin to retrace your path back to Wood Lake.

You will be paddling on large lakes most of the time, with a few delightful exceptions. Motors are not permitted on only four small lakes, and most of the route is very heavily traveled.

DAY 1: P. 196 rods, **Wood Lake,** p. 72 rods, **Hula Lake,** p. 110 rods, **Good Lake,** p. 2 rods, **Good Creek, Hoist Bay, Basswood Lake.** Campsites are plentiful along the south shore of Basswood. Don't camp north of the international border unless you have received clearance from Canadian Customs.

DAY 2: **Basswood Lake, Bayley Bay,** p. 20 rods, **Sucker Lake, Birch Lake,** p. 100 rods, **Frog Lake,** p. 70 rods, **Trident Lake.** You'll pass Canadian Customs at the 20-rod portage from Bayley Bay into Sucker Lake. Stay close to the left shore of Sucker, so you don't miss the narrow channel into Birch Lake. The two portages between Birch and Trident lakes are not well-used, and you will find Frog and Trident lakes to be a peacefully pleasant change from the busy lakes on either side.

DAY 3: **Trident Lake,** p. 120 rods, **Ensign Lake, Splash Lake,** p. 35 rods, **New Found Lake, Moose Lake,** p. 170 rods, **Wind lake.** The portage into Wind Lake is certainly the most difficult trek of the entire trip. It climbs nearly 80 feet and is over ½ mile long. Because of it, however, Wind Lake is considerably more peaceful than either Moose or Basswood Lake.

DAY 4: **Wind Lake,** p. 170 rods, **Wind Bay, Basswood Lake, Hoist Bay, Good Creek,** p. 2 rods, **Good Lake,** p. 110 rods, **Hula Lake,** p. 72 rods, **Wood Lake,** p. 196 rods. The half-mile path leading out of Wind Lake is downhill, and not as difficult as the one leading into the lake at the other end. You'll find the entrance to Good Creek just east of the busy 4-Mile Truck Portage station on the south shore of Hoist Bay. From that point on, the route should look familiar to you.

Entry Point 27—Snowbank Lake

Permits: 1003
Popularity Rank: 11
Daily Quota: 6

Location: Snowbank Lake is located about 20 miles northeast of Ely, 3 miles south of the Canadian border. To get there, follow the Fernberg Road for 18 miles from the Voyageur Visitor Center to the Snowbank Lake Road. Turn left here and drive carefully on this narrow, winding gravel road for about 4 miles to the public landing, providing access to the southeast end of Snowbank Lake. En route, you'll pass three private roads leading to resorts. At each of these intersections bear to the right, and stay on the county road to its end.

Description: A public campground at Fall Lake, 17 miles closer to Ely, just north of the Fernberg Road via Forest Route 551, provides a good place to spend the night before your trip.

Snowbank Lake has four active resorts along its southern shoreline. Fishermen base themselves at these resorts and fish during the days in Snowbank and its neighbors. Barely more than half of the travel permits for this entry point are issued to groups using canoes without motors, so you will not find much peace and quiet in the immediate vicinity of this beautiful big lake.

A long-time favorite among anglers, Snowbank contains lake trout, walleye, northern pike and bass. In recent years, however, they have become harder and harder to catch. You will probably have better luck in the neighboring lakes.

Route #33: The Disappointment Loop

3 Days, 19 Miles, 11 Lakes, 12 Portages
Difficulty: Easy
Fisher map: 113

Introduction: This little loop will take you through the chain of Snowbank's eastern neighbor lakes. From the public landing, you will paddle across the protected southern part of Snowbank to the portage into Parent Lake. From Parent, you will set a course to the northeast and wind your way through Disappointment Lake, into the chain of tiny lakes to the north, and on to popular Ensign Lake. You will travel west on this long lake for 1½ miles and then portage south to Boot Lake. After two more portages and a small pond, you will once again find yourself on Snowbank Lake. A 4-mile paddle to the southwest will return you to your origin at the public landing.

Although portages are frequent, only the one to Boot Lake is long enough to provide a challenge. Motors are permitted on all but one of the lakes, but you will not see or hear many in the chain of small lakes between Disappointment and Ensign. A group of strong canoeists could complete this route in one day.

Popular among fishermen, Ensign Lake contains northern pike, walleye and bass. Not as common in this part of the country are the rainbow trout and brook trout that have been stocked in Ahsub Lake, just north of Disappointment.

Although this route is not long, you will surely find a good deal of variety here, from tiny, shallow lakes like Jitterbug to the wide open expanse of Snowbank Lake, as deep as 140 feet.

The water level will not present a serious problem on this route, but low water can alter the complexion of the smaller lakes between Disappointment and Ensign. When it does, stumps and rocks protrude from the botton of Cattyman Lake, and the landing for the portage from Jitterbug to Ahsub extends for several more rods out into the marshy lake. At such times, in fact, Jitterbug is scarcely more than a foot deep at any point.

DAY 1: **Snowbank Lake,** p. 80 rods, **Parent Lake,** p. 85 rods, **Disappointment Lake.** Take your time paddling across Parent Lake and fish for one of the walleye that are known to inhabit it. The two portages are easy.

DAY 2: **Disappointment Lake,** p. 25 rods, **Ahsub Lake,** p. 15 rods, **Jitterbug Lake,** p. 40 rods, **Adventure Lake,** p. 10 rods, **Cattyman Lake,** p. 25 rods, **Gibson Lake,** p. 105 rods, **Ashigan Lake,** p. 53 rods, **Ensign Lake.** When the water level is high enough, you may be able to paddle through the channel connecting Adventure and Cattyman lakes, eliminating the 10-rod portage. Your first two portages this day are uphill, but the rest are downhill.

Day 3: **Ensign Lake,** p. 220 rods, **Boot Lake,** p. 30 rods, **pond,** p. 50 rods, **Snowbank Lake.** On this day you will be portaging uphill, gaining 80 feet from Ensign to Snowbank Lake. If the wind is strong out of the west, good luck! If so, you may want to settle down in the campsite just south of the portage in the northeast corner of Snowbank, and wait until the winds subside later in the evening.

ute #34: The Lake Trout Route

) Miles, 39 Lakes, 1 Creek, 48 Portages
Difficulty: Challenging
Fisher map: 113

Introduction: This wilderness route first follows the motor route from Snowbank Lake east and north through Disappointment Lake to Ima Lake. Continuing along the motor route, you will paddle southeast through Hatchet and into Thomas Lake, where you will turn back to the northeast and leave the motorboats behind. From Fraser Lake you will continue east and enter into an interior portion of the BWCA that is seldom visited by other canoeists. A series of tiny lakes and long portages will lead you eventually to popular Little Saganaga Lake. From Little Sag you will point your course northwest and paddle through beautiful big Gabimichigami Lake and across a lovely series of pools and rapids that drain into another popular lake, Ogishkemuncie. Through a chain of small lakes and even tinier ponds, you will continue moving west, into impressive, cliff-lined Kekekabic Lake and then north through Pickle, Spoon and Bonnie lakes to Knife Lake, on the international border. You will follow this long, clear border lake southwest to its end, and beyond to Vera and Ensign lakes. After three more portages to the south, you will find yourself back on familiar Snowbank Lake. Four miles of paddling across this big lake will return you to your origin at the public landing on the south shore.

Although this route starts and ends on busy motor routes, motors are prohibited from most of the loop. Your third day will take you through the most remote interior portion of all the BWCA, where you will see only dedicated wilderness canoeists like yourself. Attractive scenery exists all along the way, but the part of the route between Little Saganaga Lake and Kekekabic Lake is truly exceptional. Nowhere will you find scenery more beautiful!

If you are an angler in search of lake trout, you will have a golden opportunity to catch them on this trip. This species is known to inhabit Snowbank, Thomas, Little Saganaga, Gabimichigami, Kekekabic and Knife lakes. And you will also find northern pike and walleye in Ima, Fraser, Vera, Ensign and other lakes en route.

DAY 1: **Snowbank Lake,** p. 80 rods, **Parent Lake,** p. 85 rods, **Disappointment Lake,** p. 25 rods, **Ahsub Lake,** p. 15 rods, **Jitterbug Lake,** p. 40 rods, **Adventure Lake,** p. 10 rods, **Cattyman Lake,** p. 55 rods, **Jordan Lake,** p. 5 rods,

Ima Lake. Although five of these portages are uphill, none are difficult. When the water level is high enough, you may be able to paddle through the channel connecting Adventure and Cattyman lakes, eliminating the 10-rod portage.

DAY 2: **Ima Lake,** p. 50 rods, **Hatchet Lake,** p. 10 rods, **creek,** p. 10 rods, **creek,** p. 10 rods, **pond,** p. 5 rods, **Thomas Lake, Fraser Lake,** p. 65 rods, **Sagus Lake.** Under normal water conditions, you can probably pull your canoe up through the first two rapids in the creek between Thomas and Hatchet lakes, eliminating two 10-rod portages. The third short carry crosses the famed Kekekabic Trail. Motors are not allowed beyond Thomas Lake.

DAY 3: **Sagus Lake,** p. 42 rods, **Roe Lake,** p. 60 rods, **Cap Lake,** p. 190 rods, **Ledge Lake,** p. 160 rods, **Vee Lake,** p. 80 rods, **lake,** p. 40 rods, **Hoe Lake,** p. 100 rods, **Makwa Lake,** p. 45 rods, **Elton Lake,** p. 19 rods, **pond,** p. 19 rods, **Little Saganaga Lake.** You will surely look back at this day as your roughest of the whole trip. Few people penetrate this remote portion of the BWCA, and for the first time along this route you will sense a feeling of true wilderness solitude.

DAY 4: **Little Saganaga Lake,** p. 30 rods, **Rattle Lake,** p. 25 rods, **Gabimichigami Lake,** p. 15 rods, **Agamok Lake,** 3 portages, **Mueller Lake,** p. 80 rods, **Ogishkemuncie Lake.** This area must rank as one of the most beautiful in the North Woods, from island-studded Little Saganaga, to wide-open Gabimichigami, to the sheltered little pools and rapids between Mueller and Agamok lakes. It is possible to portage directly from Agamok to Mueller via a 100-rod trail, but in doing so you would miss the lovely series of pools, rapids and a scenic waterfall. Instead, I recommend the three short, rocky portages, which are steep in places but not longer than 20 rods. The final portage of the day is steep, but mostly downhill, from Mueller to Ogishkemuncie Lake. This is a very popular lake, so find your campsite early!

DAY 5: **Ogishkemuncie Lake,** p. 15 rods, **Annie Lake,** p. 15 rods, **Lake Jean,** p. 15 rods, **Eddy Lake,** 5 portages, **Kekekabic Lake,** p. 80 rods, **Pickle Lake,** p. 25 rods, **Spoon Lake.** The five portages between Eddy and Kekekabic lakes join a series of tiny pools, known as the Kekekabic Ponds. All the carries are short and quite easy, but they may slow your progress considerably. Kekekabic Lake is nothing less than spectacular when you enter it from the ponds. As you emerge from the narrow east end, scenic bluffs tower above your canoe, and along the distant southern shoreline hills rise to 400 feet above the lake. Ahead of you lie over four miles of scenic lake shore — most impressive after the chain of little ponds from which you came.

DAY 6: **Spoon Lake,** p. 25 rods, **Bonnie Lake,** p. 33 rods, **Knife Lake,** p. 200 rods, **Vera Lake.** You may wish to visit Isle of Pines at the southwest end of Knife Lake, where Dorothy Molter operates a trading post and sells home-made root beer to thirsty travelers. Formerly a nurse in Chicago, Dorothy has lived on these three islands for over 40 years. You will find her a delight to visit with, but please respect her private property. The 200-rod portage into Vera Lake is a tough one, climbing steeply to 80 feet above Knife Lake, before dropping 70 feet to Vera Lake. Bears are common in the area, so prepare.

DAY 7: **Vera Lake,** p. 180 rods, **Ensign Lake,** p. 220 rods, **Boot Lake,** p. 30 rods, **pond,** p. 50 rods, **Snowbank Lake.** (See comments for Day 3, Route #33.)

Entry Point 30—Lake One

Permits: 2586
Popularity Rank: 4
Daily Quota: 17

Location: Lake One is seventeen miles straight east of Ely. To get there, follow the Fernberg Road for 19 miles from the Voyageur Visitor Center to its end. A large parking lot is adjacent to the nice public landing.

Description: Camping is prohibited at the landing. A National Forest Campground is located next to Fall Lake, 14 miles closer to Ely on the Fernberg Road, a good place to spend the night before your trip.

This entry point serves a very popular designated motor route into the interior of the Boundary Waters, as far east as Alice Lake and north to the Canadian border. Nevertheless, most motorists confine themselves to the immediate vicinity of Lake One. Two thirds of the travel permits are issued to parties using canoes without motors.

Route #35: The Clearwater-Kawishiwi Loop

3 Days, 28 Miles, 8 Lakes, 1 River, 14 Portages
Difficulty: Challenging
Fisher map: 112

Introduction: This little loop will take you southeast through Lake One and into Lake Two. Then you will leave this busy motor route and paddle south into a part of the BWCA that receives light use, from Rock Island Lake to Turtle Lake. From Turtle, you will portage into the southernmost motor route through the Boundary Waters, and follow it northwest from Bald Eagle Lake to the South Kawishiwi River. You will walk your canoe up the shallow rapids and paddle through the quiet pools of the Kawishiwi, following its course northeast to the public landing on Lake One.

Although the beginning of this route receives heavy use, the remainder receives only light to moderate travel. Motors are allowed on all but the three remote lakes between Lake Two and Bald Eagle.

Fishermen will find walleye, northern pike, bass and pan fish throughout much of the route.

DAY 1: **Lake One,** p. 30 rods, **pond,** p. 45 rods, **Lake Two,** p. 65 rods, **Rock Island Lake,** p. 242 rods, **Clearwater**

Lake. This last, long portage is relatively level most of the way, but downhill at the end, where a nice sandy beach greets you. Clearwater Lake is aptly named, and you will find several nice campsites along its north shore. Try fishing for walleye here.

You may find this trip's route confusing from the beginning. Lake One, with its many islands and meandering bays, offers a sporty challenge to the map reader. From the landing, first bear to the left and then to the right, as you pass through a very narrow channel that passes Kawishiwi Lodge en route to the main body of the lake. If confused by the many islands in the lake, use your compass and common sense, and don't treat the map as "gospel." Things won't look the way you think they should!

DAY 2: **Clearwater Lake,** p. 252 rods, **Turtle Lake,** p. 186 rods, **Bald Eagle Lake, rapids, Gabbro Lake, Little Gabbro Lake,** p. 122 rods, **South Kawishiwi River.** Your first long portage is nearly level and nothing to worry about. The second, on the other hand, climbs steeply uphill from Turtle Lake before descending to Bald Eagle Lake. The short, swift rapids between Bald Eagle and Gabbro lakes can be easily shot in your canoe.

DAY 3: **South Kawishiwi River,** p. 28 rods, **river,** p. 18 rods, **river,** p. 12 rods, **river,** p. 8 rods, **river,** p. 40 rods, **river,** p. 20 rods, **river,** p. 19 rods, **Lake One.** With normal water conditions, you may eliminate four of the portages along the Kawishiwi River by walking your canoe up the shallow rapids. The only two that must be portaged around are at the 8-rod and the 40-rod trails. Make certain that your last carry is the 19-rod path to Lake One. It is an easy mistake to take the 25-rod trail to Confusion Lake instead. Continue past the first portage that you pass on the right around a small island to the portage at the east end of the tiny bay.

Route #36: The Alice-Thomas Route

5 Days, 55 Miles, 26 Lakes, 1 River, 2 Creeks, 32 Portages
Difficulty: Challenging
Fisher map: 113

Introduction: This interesting loop follows motor routes much of the way. But it also penetrates the remote interior portion of the Boundary Waters where motors are not allowed and where few canoeists travel. From Lake One, you will paddle southeast through Lakes Two, Three and Four to the island-studded bays of beautiful Lake Insula. From the north end of Insula, you will continue northeast up the Kawishiwi River, then north through Elbow and Adams lakes, and camp on isolated Boulder Lake, your farthest point east. Turning back to the west, you will paddle through Fraser and Thomas lakes, portage across the Kekekabic Trail, and float down the shallow stream to Ima Lake. From Ima, you will travel southwest through the tiny lakes leading to Disappointment, Parent and Snowbank lakes. Your canoe trip will end at the public landing on Snowbank Lake, five miles by road from your origin at the Lake One Landing. Unless you have made arrangements to have a vehicle waiting, your trip will end with a five-mile hike.

All along this route, fishing is good for northern pike and walleye. Lake trout are also found in Thomas and Snowbank lakes. The largest fish I have caught was pulled from the Kawishiwi River east of Lake Insula — a northern pike that stole three lures before he finally met his match.

DAY 1: **Lake One,** p. 30 rods, **pond,** p. 45 rods, **Lake Two, Lake Three, Lake Four,** p. 20 rods, **Kawishiwi River,** p. 25 rods, **river,** p. 10 rods, **river, Hudson Lake.** (See comments for Day 1, Route #35.) You will see many other travelers this day, but most of the motorboats go no farther than the numbered lakes. In spite of the traffic, I have seen moose in the southernmost bay of Hudson Lake.

DAY 2: **Hudson Lake,** p. 105 rods, **Lake Insula,** p. 18 rods, **Kawishiwi River, Alice Lake,** p. 20 rods, **Kawishiwi River,** p. 90 rods, **river.** The southwest end of Lake Insula may be confusing to even an experienced map reader. Use your compass, if necessary, and follow a general heading, instead of trying to account for every little island you see. You will find a display of Indian rock paintings south of your last portage this day, on the west shore of the Kawishiwi River. Several good campsites are nearby.

DAY 3: **Kawishiwi River,** p. 15 rods, **river,** p. 15 rods, **lake,** p. 30 rods, **Elbow Lake,** p. 90 rods, **Adams Lake, creek,** p. 15 rods, **creek, Boulder Lake.** You will see few, if any, other people after you veer north from the Kawishiwi River. Between Adams and Boulder lakes, there may be a couple of liftovers, in addition to the 15-rod portage.

DAY 4: **Boulder Lake,** p. 220 rods, **Cap Lake,** p. 60 rods, **Roe Lake,** p. 42 rods, **Sagus Lake,** p. 65 rods, **Fraser Lake, Thomas Lake,** p. 5 rods, **pond,** p. 10 rods, **creek,** p. 10 rods, **creek,** p. 10 rods, **Hatchet Lake,** p. 50 rods, **Ima Lake.** Your first long portage will split after 135 rods of hiking. The right trail leads to Ledge Lake, so bear to the left for 85 more rods to

Cap Lake. Upon entering Thomas Lake, you will again be following a motor route, and traffic will increase. If the water level is not too low, the second and third 10-rod portages between Thomas and Hatchet lakes may be eliminated by walking or lining your canoe down the shallow rapids. Ima Lake is a popular one, so find a campsite as early as possible.

DAY 5: **Ima Lake,** p. 5 rods, **Jordan Lake,** p. 55 rods, **Cattyman Lake,** p. 10 rods, **Adventure Lake,** p. 40 rods, **Jitterbug Lake,** p. 15 rods, **Ahsub Lake,** p. 25 rods, **Disappointment Lake,** p. 85 rods, **Parent Lake,** p. 80 rods, **Snowbank Lake.** If the water level is high enough, you may be able to eliminate the 10-rod portage between Cattyman and Adventure lakes by paddling through the interconnecting channel. Rainbow trout and brook trout are stocked in Ahsub Lake, and Parent Lake is known for its good walleye fishing.

Entry Point 31 —Farm Lake

Permits: 516
Popularity Rank: 21
Daily Quota: 3

  Location: Farm Lake is located straight east of Ely, about 5 miles away. To get there, follow State Highway 169 one mile from the Voyageur Visitor Center to its intersection with County Road 58-16. Follow this road for 3 miles to the public access on the left side of the road, 1 mile after the road becomes gravel.

  Description: A public campground at nearby Fall Lake is a good place to spend the night before your trip. It is reached via the Fall Lake Road, which meets the Fernberg Road 5 miles east of the Voyageur Visitor Center.

  Farm Lake, located entirely outside the BWCA, is decorated with resorts and private cabins along the southern and western shorelines. It is not a heavily used entry point even though it serves a designated motor route, and a good deal of solitude and relative isolation can be had at several lakes within easy reach.

Route #37: The Clearwater-Turtle Loop

4 Days, 40 Miles, 11 Lakes, 2 Rivers, 19 Portages
Difficulty: Challenging
Fisher map: 112

  Introduction: This interesting route will take you through some of the busiest and also some of the least traveled lakes in the BWCA, as well as through portions of the mellow Kawishiwi River. From Farm Lake you will paddle east into the North Kawishiwi River, along the border of the Boundary Waters to Lakes One and Two. Leaving these heavily used lakes, you will then turn south and portage into peaceful lakes where motors are prohibited. Then you will return to a motor route at Bald Eagle Lake and journey northwest through Gabbro and Little Gabbro lakes to the South Kawishiwi River. After paddling through Clear Lake you will return to the North Kawishiwi River and retrace your strokes to the public landing at Farm Lake.

  Although most of the route is open to motor traffic, the only place where it may be a disturbance is in the vicinity of Lake One, the seventh busiest entry point in the BWCA. Not far away, however, you will experience true wilderness solitude during your night on Clearwater Lake. Gentle rapids and quiest pools, large open lakes and generally good fishing all combine to make this route a great one. Walleye and northern pike are prevalent throughout.

DAY 1: **Farm Lake, North Kawishiwi River,** p. 10 rods, **river,** p. 10 rods, **river,** p. 18 rods, **river,** p. 210 rods, **river.** The first 10-rod portage is necessary only during periods of very low water; normally you can paddle right up the channel. The other two short rapids can be easily walked up or lined. But psych up for the 210-rod portage — it's rough! The path is not well-used and it is nearly all uphill, gaining almost 100 feet in elevation. You'll find two splendid campsites just before the junction of the North and South Kawishiwi rivers, both with ample space for large groups.

DAY 2: **Kawishiwi River,** p. 8 rods, **river,** p. 40 rods, **river,** p. 20 rods, **river,** p. 25 rods, **Confusion Lake,** p. 41 rods, **Lake One,** p. 30 rods, **pond,** p. 45 rods, **Lake Two,** p. 65 rods, **Rock Island Lake,** p. 242 rods, **Clearwater Lake.** If you prefer walking up rapids to carrying all your gear overland, the 20-rod portage along the Kawishiwi River is usually no problem. But resist the temptation to walk up the two rapids before it. The 8-rod portage bypasses a small waterfall, and the 40-rod path goes around what appears from the bottom to be "just another pretty rapids" but becomes swifter and deeper the farther up you get, and at the top you are greeted by a small dam. I once pulled through it with empty canoes — just barely — but I would never attempt it with a loaded craft. Don't worry about the 242-rod portage. It is the second longest carry of the trip, but mostly level.

DAY 3: **Clearwater Lake,** p. 252 rods, **Turtle Lake,** p. 186 rods, **Bald Eagle Lake, rapids, Gabbro Lake, Little Gabbro Lake,** p. 122 rods, **South Kawishiwi River, rapids, River,** p. 70 rods, **Clear Lake.** Your first two portages are long and not very well-traveled, but not very difficult either. The 252-rod path from Clearwater to Turtle is virtually level. The 186-rod trail into Bald Eagle, on the other hand, begins rather steeply uphill, but then descends most of the way. You will have no trouble shooting through the small rapids between Bald Eagle and Gabbro lakes and on the South Kawishiwi River. Clear Lake is a serene and pretty little lake that offers good northern pike fishing.

DAY 4: **Clear Lake,** p. 144 rods, **North Kawishiwi River,** p. 10 rods, **river, Farm Lake.** As on the first day, the 10-rod portage on the Kawishiwi River may not be necessary unless the water level is extremely low.

Ch. 5:
Entry from State Highway 1

The South-Central Region

Five entry points are accessible from State Highway 1 southeast of Ely, but only one — South Kawishiwi River — is easily accessible. Four of the points require extensive back-woods driving on county roads and forest routes — gravel for many miles.

To get to these entry points, simply follow Highway 1 south from Ely. The South Kawishiwi River entry point is just off the highway. The other four are reached from the little town of Isabella, located about halfway between Ely and Lake Superior on Highway 1.

The highway is usually quite good, but it does wind considerably and is rather hilly at times.

Entry Point 32—South Kawishiwi River

Permits: 302
Popularity Rank: 30
Daily Quota: 3

Location: Public access to the Kawishiwi River is located 8 miles southeast of Ely. To drive there, follow State Highway 1 12 miles southeast of Ely, 1000 feet past the river bridge.

Description: The Forest Service Kawishiwi Campground, with public swimming beach and parking lot, is adjacent to the boat access. It is an excellent place to spend the night before your journey into the Boundary Waters Canoe Area.

Entry points #29-North Kawishiwi River and #33-Nickel Creek are classified with the South Kawishiwi River for the purpose of quota restrictions. Only three parties are allowed to enter the BWCA from all three of these entry points combined. Since all three serve the same general region, I have included only the most popular and most easily accessible in this guide.

The Kawishiwi is a shallow, wide, rocky-bottomed series of pools and rapids. Red pine, balsam, cedar and spruce populate its shore, and walleye and northern pike inhabit its depths. Good campsites are found all along its course, wherever a rocky outcropping exists. Under normal water conditions, many of the portages en route may be avoided by walking, lining or running your canoe through the accompanying whitewater. The portages may be more desirable, however, when the water is low or the day is cool.

Although the Kawishiwi River is a designated motor route, nearly two thirds of the parties entering the BWCA here use canoes without motors.

Route #38: The Split River Route

3 Days, 30 Miles, 1 Lake, 2 Rivers, 18 Portages
Difficulty: Challenging
Fisher map: 112

Introduction: This short loop will take you up the South Kawishiwi River to its junction with the North Kawishiwi River. You will then paddle to the west down this scenic river until you reach the portage to Clear Lake. Beyond Clear Lake, you'll re-enter the South Kawishiwi River and follow it back to your origin at Highway 1.

The entire route is open to motor traffic, but seldom is it a nuisance. If the water level is appropriate, you will have an excellent opportunity to shoot through several small rapids, as well as to walk your canoe up many more. A good group of competent paddlers could easily complete this route in two days. But stretch it into three days and take time to appreciate the natural beauty that surrounds you.

DAY 1: **South Kawishiwi River,** p. 68 rods, **river,** p. 29 rods, **river,** p. 30 rods, **river,** p. 67 rods, **river,** p. 7 rods, **river.** You can avoid all of the portages this day by walking your canoe up the accompanying rapids.

DAY 2: **South Kawishiwi River, rapids, river,** p. 28 rods, **river,** p. 18 rods, **river,** p. 12 rods, **North Kawishiwi River,** p. 210 rods, **river,** p. 18 rods, **river,** p. 10 rods, **river,** p. 144 rods, **Clear Lake.** Again, you will be able to walk your canoe up all the rapids on the South Kawishiwi River this day. Unfortunately, the 210-rod portage must be taken, because the river drops 60 feet in ½ mile. The trail is not heavily used, but it is primarily downhill, so it should not cause you too much difficulty.

DAY 3: **Clear Lake,** p. 70 rods, **South Kawishiwi River,** p. 7 rods, **river,** p. 67 rods, **river,** p. 30 rods, **river,** p. 29 rods, **river,** p. 68 rods, **river.** After the initial 70-rod portage, you can eliminate all of the other portages by walking, lining or running the shallow rapids, depending on the water conditions and your whitewater skills.

Route #39: The Bald Eagle-Gull Route

5 Days, 46 Miles, 11 Lakes, 1 River, 1 Creek, 29 Portages.
Difficulty: Challenging
Fisher map: 112

Introduction: This interesting route will take you through some of the busiest and some of the *least* traveled lakes in the BWCA as well as through all of the south branch of the Kawishiwi River. You will paddle northeast up the South Kawishiwi River to the portage into Little Gabbro Lake, then southeast through Gabbro and Bald Eagle lakes. Leaving the motor route, you'll head north into a chain of lakes that sees far fewer people and requires considerably more portaging. At Lake Two you'll point west and make your return trip through Lake One and down the Kawishiwi River, then into the south branch from which you came. Although most of the route is open to motors, the only place where they may be a disturbance is in the vicinity of Lake One, the fourth busiest entry point in the BWCA. The region between Lake Two and Bald Eagle is closed to motors, and here you will experience the essence of wilderness solitude. Gentle rapids and quiet pools, large open lakes and generally good fishing all combine to make this route a great one. Walleye and northern pike are prevalent throughout.

DAY 1: **South Kawishiwi River,** p. 68 rods, **river,** p. 29 rods, **river,** p. 30 rods, **river,** p. 67 rods, **river,** p. 7 rods, **river.** You can avoid all the portages this day by walking your canoe up the accompanying rapids.

DAY 2: **South Kawishiwi River, rapids, river,** p. 122 rods, **Little Gabbro Lake, Gabbro Lake,** p. 2-5 rods, **Bald Eagle Lake,** p. 189 rods, **Gull Creek,** p. 41 rods, **Gull Lake.** The true adventurer with time to kill can avoid the 122-rod portage from the South Kawishiwi River to Little Gabbro Lake by walking up two sets of gentle rapids, and portaging a small falls and an old logging dam. The map won't show this, so here is what to look for: just beyond the north end of the 122-rod portage you'll encounter a short stretch of rapids that must be walked up (no portage). Bearing to the left shoreline, you'll soon come to a picturesque little waterfall that must be passed on the left by a steep, overgrown 10-rod portage that appears to have been used only once or twice since the last Chippewa Indians moved out of the region. Soon after, you will again have to walk up a somewhat longer stretch of rapids, until you arrive at the old dam, which can be passed on the right via an even less traveled path. *Voila:* the back door to Little Gabbro Lake. It is kind of fun, but takes much longer than the 122-rod portage.

Beware the 189-rod portage out of Bald Eagle Lake. It is mostly uphill, climbing to 90 feet above the lake. Several campsites await you on Gull Lake, but most are out of the way.

DAY 3: **Gull Lake,** p. 50 rods, **Pietro Lake,** p. 64 rods, **Camdre Lake,** p. 125 rods, **Clearwater Lake,** p. 242 rods, **Rock Island Lake,** p. 65 rods, **Lake Two.** The only notably uphill trek of this day is the 64-rod portage from Pietro to Camdre Lake. The long 242-rod trail out of Clearwater Lake has a steep uphill portion at the beginning, but it soon levels off and does not present a major challenge.

DAY 4: **Lake Two,** p. 45 rods, **pond,** p. 30 rods, **Lake One,** p. 41 rods, **Confusion Lake,** p. 25 rods, **Kawishiwi River,** p. 20 rods, **river,** p. 40 rods, **river,** p. 8 rods, **river, South Kawishiwi River,** p. 12 rods, **river,** p. 18 rods, **river,** p. 28 rods, **river, rapids, river.** For those who prefer a little

whitewater to the drudgery of portaging, four of the six portages on the Kawishiwi River this day may be avoided (20, 12,
18 and 28 rods) by shooting, lining or walking the respective
rapids, depending on the water depth. Be sure to check them
out first, because, although the rapids are not considered
dangerous, sharp rocks could damage your canoe.

DAY 5: **South Kawishiwi River,** p. 7 rods, **river,** p. 67
rods, **river,** p. 30 rods, **river,** p. 29 rods, **river,** p. 68 rods, **river.**
Again, you can eliminate all other portages this day by walk-
ing, lining, or running the shallow rapids, if the water level is
right.

Entry Point 34—Island River

Permits: 143
Popularity Rank: 43
Daily Quota: 4

Location: The Island River entry point is located 28 miles southeast of Ely. From Isabella on State Highway 1, follow Forest Route 172 one mile east to Forest Route 369. Turn left and follow 369 north for about 6 miles to Forest Route 373 and follow it another 6 miles northwest to Forest Route 377. Turn right and follow 377 4½ miles to the Island River bridge, which is located *just* off the bottom of Fisher's map#113.

Description: Several National Forest Campgrounds are located along State Highway 1, providing places to spend the night before your trip. Coming from Ely, you will pass campgrounds at the South Kawishiwi River, McDougal Lakes and Little Isabella River. The closest, however, is at Dumbbell Lake, about 3 miles out of your way, on Forest Route 172, 4 miles east of Isabella.

High-quality wilderness canoe trips can be taken from the Island River entry point. The Island and Isabella river valleys teem with wildlife, including moose and bald eagles. Both are scenic rivers with occasional white water and little canoe traffic. You will be well-rewarded for the extra driving time it takes to get there.

Route #40: The Isabella-
South Kawishiwi Rivers Loop

5 Days, 57 Miles, 12 Lakes, 3 Rivers, 1 Creek, 37 Portages
Difficulty: Challenging
Fisher maps: 112, 113

Introduction: This fascinating route will take you on three of the prettiest rivers in the BWCA. You will also visit several lakes that are seldom visited by others, as well as two of the most heavily used lakes in the Boundary Waters. From Forest Route 377, you will paddle for only a couple of miles down the Island River before entering the Isabella River. You'll continue on down this placid, forest-lined stream to Bald Eagle Lake. From this popular lake you will head north through Gull to Clearwater and on to popular Lakes One and Two. From near the busy Lake One landing you will turn west and paddle down the scenic North Kawishiwi River, and then follow the South branch to Little Gabbro Lake. Beyond Gabbro and Bald Eagle lakes, you will then retrace your path up the Isabella and Island rivers to your origin at Forest Route 377. Motors are permitted along the western part of this route, but the only place where they may become a nuisance is on Lakes One and Two. Although this route requires that you paddle through the Isabella and Island rivers twice, I'm sure its attractiveness will make it worth while.

Fishing for walleye is possible throughout most of the route. You will also find northern pike, bass and pan fish in Lakes One and Two, Gabbro, Bald Eagle and the South Kawishiwi and Isabella rivers. It will take five full days to complete this challenging route. If fishing is your main purpose, you may wish to stretch it into six days. Strong trippers, however, could make it in four.

DAY 1: **Island River,** p. 11 rods, **river,** p. 10 rods, **river, Isabella River,** p. 130 rods, **river, Rice Lake, Isabella River,** p. 10 rods, **river,** p. 27 rods, **river,** p. 27 rods, **river,** p. 40 rods, **river,** p. 40 rods, **river, rapids, river,** p. 190 rods, **Bald Eagle Lake.** Your first day will be a long one, but you should make fairly good time paddling down the two rivers. Though not extremely swift, the current is noticeable. And two or three of the shorter rapids may be safely shot if the water level is sufficiently high. ALWAYS check them out first! I found an abandoned fiberglass canoe at the base of one of the longer rapids, overturned on a large rock with a fist-sized hole punched out of the bottom. Chances are, the owner didn't look first. . . . On the same trip, I also saw three moose along the Isabella River. This is a good route for seeing wildlife.

DAY 2: **Bald Eagle Lake,** p. 189 rods, **Gull Creek,** p. 41 rods, **Gull Lake,** p. 50 rods, **Pietro Lake,** p. 64 rods, **Camdre Lake,** p. 125 rods, **Clearwater Lake.** This day will be much easier than the first, so as to end at Clearwater. If you prefer to spend your nights on peaceful, isolated lakes, you will surely enjoy Clearwater Lake much more than Lake Two. There is a campsite on Rock Island Lake, but only one, and after you cross the 242-rod portage from Clearwater Lake, you are committed to continue on. The only major portage of the day is your first, a 189-rod uphill trek that climbs over a 90-foot hill. The only other uphill path is the 64-rod trail from Pietro to Camdre Lake. You'll find a nice sandy beach for swimming at the portage leading to Rock Island Lake. A good campsite is close by on the northeast shore.

DAY 3: **Clearwater Lake,** p. 242 rods, **Rock Island**

Lake, p. 65 rods, **Lake Two,** p. 45 rods, **pond,** p. 30 rods, **Lake One,** p. 41 rods, **Confusion Lake,** p. 25 rods, **Kawishiwi River,** p. 20 rods, **river,** p. 40 rods, **river,** p. 8 rods, **river.** The 242-rod portage out of Clearwater Lake has a steep uphill portion at the beginning, but it soon levels off and does not present a major challenge. You will probably see many motor boats on the busy motor route through lakes One and Two. The Kawishiwi River is also a motor route, but it will be much more peaceful. You should be able to walk, line or shoot your canoe down the first set of rapids on the river, eliminating the 20-rod portage. Two very nice campsites are found just beyond the entrance into the North Kawishiwi River, with plenty of space for the largest of groups. Should you need additional supplies or have a craving for pop and candy bars, you may wish to paddle to Kawishiwi Lodge at the north end of Lake One, just out of the Boundary Waters and less than a mile from the Lake One Landing. If you go this way, you will portage 19 rods directly from Lake One into Kawishiwi River and bypass Confusion Lake altogether. The choice is yours.

DAY 4: **Kawishiwi River, South Kawishiwi River,** p. 12 rods, **river,** p. 18 rods, **river,** p. 28 rods, **river,** p. 122 rods, **Little Gabbro Lake, Gabbro Lake,** p. 2-5 rods, **Bald Eagle Lake.** If desired you can eliminate the three portages on the Kawishiwi River by shooting, lining or walking your canoe down the white water. But be sure to check them out first, because, although the rapids are not considered dangerous, sharp rocks could damage your canoe. A small, swift rapids separates Gabbro and Bald Eagle. Your canoe could be pulled through if you prefer to avoid the short but tricky portage on the right.

DAY 5: **Bald Eagle Lake,** p. 190 rods, **Isabella River, rapids, river,** p. 40 rods, **river,** p. 40 rods, **river,** p. 27 rods, **river,** p. 27 rods, **river,** p. 10 rods, **river, Rice Lake, Isabella River,** p. 130 rods, **river, Island River,** p. 10 rods, **river,** p. 11 rods, **river.** Your last day is merely the reverse of the first, but you can count on its taking longer. Not only will you be paddling against the current but you will also have to portage around several short rapids through which you may have shot or lined your canoe going down. You may even wish to spend the night at a campsite at the junction of the Island and Isabella rivers, and then paddle the short distance to your car early the next morning.

Route #41: The Four Rivers Route

7 Days, 94 Miles, 20 Lakes, 4 Rivers, 1 Creek, 54 Portages
Difficulty: Challenging
Fisher maps: 112, 113

Introduction: This fascinating route will lead you west down the lovely Island and Isabella rivers to the base of Bald Eagle Lake. From here you will point northwest and navigate the open waters of Bald Eagle and Gabbro lakes until you intersect the South Kawishiwi River. You will paddle, pull and carry your canoe through the scenic pools and up the foaming white water of the Kawishiwi River, across the popular "numbered lakes" and into island-studded Lake Insula. On up the Kawishiwi River you will pause to view a display of old Indian rock paintings decorating the vertical cliffs along its shore. At Malberg Lake you will turn south and continue on up the system of lakes, ponds and creeks that compose the upper reaches of the Kawishiwi River, until you reach its source at Kawishiwi Lake. From there, a 2-mile trek on Forest Route 354 will take you to the winding wilderness of Hog Creek and Perent Lake beyond. Across Perent Lake you will enter the pristine wilderness of the Perent River, along whose shores moose abound. Then into Isabella Lake you will paddle, and at the other side you will re-enter the Isabella River and follow it to the familiar waters of the Island River from which you emerged a week earlier.

Wildlife is plentiful along this scenic route. Countless beaver homes decorate the scenic banks of the Kawishiwi River. In addition, a high-density moose population exists in the southeast part of this trip. In the early summer of 1977, my wife and I saw eight moose along the way, and fresh tracks were frequently seen on portage trails beside the Perent River.

Fishing is generally excellent throughout the loop. Walleye and northern pike, in particular, are plentiful in Perent and Isabella lakes, in all parts of the Kawishiwi River and in such lakes as Malberg, Koma and Polly. Crappies and bass may also be found in several of the lakes. Much of this route is open to motor traffic, including all the Kawishiwi system from the South Kawishiwi River through Alice Lake, as well as Hog Creek, Perent, Isabella, Bald Eagle and Gabbro lakes. The region around Lake One is very heavily used during much of the summer, and the Kawishiwi-Polly-Malberg chain of lakes is also very popular. But the variety of beautiful scenery that exists along the "Four Rivers Route" more than compensates for the number of people encountered along the way. A good blend of large and small lakes with rivers and tiny creeks eliminates any chance of boredom. Although portages are frequent, most are quite short and easily traversed; the longest is 190 rods.

Allow seven full days to complete this challenging route. Eight would permit more time to fish. An experienced crew of strong paddlers could complete the route in six days, or even less. Low water and occasional beaver dams may slow travel considerably, especially on the Perent River and Hog Creek, as well as eliminate the possibilitiy of running rapids on the Isabella River.

DAY 1: **Island River,** p. 11 rods, **river,** p. 10 rods, **river, Isabella River,** p. 130 rods, **river, Rice Lake, Isabella River,** p. 10 rods, **river,** p. 27 rods, **river,** p. 27 rods, **river,** p. 40 rods, **river,** p. 40 rods, **river, rapids, river,** p. 190 rods, **Bald Eagle Lake.** (See comments for Day 1, Route #40.)

DAY 2: **Bald Eagle Lake, rapids, Gabbro Lake, Little Gabbro Lake,** p. 122 rods, **South Kawishiwi River,** p. 28 rods, **river,** p. 18 rods, **river,** p. 12 rods, **Kawishiwi River,** p. 8 rods, **river,** p. 40 rods, **river,** p. 20 rods, **river,** p. 19 rods, **Lake One.** A short swift rapids in the narrows between Bald Eagle and Gabbro lakes can be easily and safely run. And if the sun is bright and the air is warm, you may wish to eliminate all but two of the portages on the South Kawishiwi River. The first three rapids that you encounter (28, 18 and 12 rods) can be walked up with little difficulty in normal to low water, or lined up during periods of higher water. So can the last rapids (20 rods) before the portage into Lake One. You had better resist the temptation to walk up the white water bypassed by the 8-rod and 40-rod portages, however. The first one is a small waterfall. The longer one begins innocently enough, but becomes progressively more difficult as the gradient increases and the rocky banks become steeper, climaxed by an old log dam at the top.

After the final portage of 19 rods into Lake One, you will soon see the public landing serving one of the busiest entry points for the BWCA. Less than a mile farther into the narrow corridor leading to the main body of Lake One, you will paddle past Kawishiwi Lodge, your only direct contact with civilization on this route.

If you wish not to blemish your wilderness experience by this direct contact, you may avoid the more popular entry route into Lake One by portaging 25 rods into Confusion Lake, followed by 41 rods into Lake One. This eliminates about three miles of paddling, but increases portaging by 47 rods.

DAY 3: **Lake One,** p. 30 rods, **pond,** p. 45 rods, **Lake Two, Lake Three, Lake Four,** p. 20 rods, **Kawishiwi River,** p. 25 rods, **river,** p. 10 rods, **river, Hudson Lake,** p. 105 rods, **Lake Insula.** You will be traveling the entire day on a heavily used motor route as you leave the sixth most popular entry point for the BWCA. If this day is Saturday, Sunday or Monday, when campsites are at a premium, you would be wise to stop early for the night.

DAY 4: **Lake Insula,** p. 18 rods, **Kawishiwi River, Alice Lake,** p. 20 rods, **Kawishiwi River,** p. 90 rods, **river,** p. 15 rods, **river,** p. 60 rods, **Malberg Lake.** Island-studded Lake Insula may provide a challenge to the novice map reader. Watch the landmarks carefully, or you may spend most of the day on this beautiful lake. If you are tired of freeze-dried and dehydrated foods by now, this day should provide an excellent opportunity to catch walleye and northern pike. Take time out for a short side trip to the Indian pictographs, located just south of the 90-rod portage after Alice Lake. A careful examination of the vertical cliffs bordering the river on the west side will yield reminders of a civilization that once flourished in this water wilderness.

DAY 5: **Malberg Lake,** p. 24 rods, **Koma Lake,** p. 127 rods, **Kawishiwi River,** p. 48 rods, **river,** p. 19 rods, **Lake Polly,** p. 91 rods, **Townline Lake,** p. 181 rods, **Kawasaschong Lake.** You won't hear motor boats this day, but canoe traffic from the Kawishiwi Lake entry point is often heavy. Nevertheless, there are plenty of campsites along the way to accommodate the traffic.

DAY 6: **Kawasaschong Lake, Kawishiwi River,** p. 11 rods, **river,** p. 20 rods, **Square Lake, Kawishiwi River, Kawishiwi Lake,** p. 640 rods, **Hog Creek,** p. 15 rods, **Hog Creek, Perent Lake.** When the water level is low, the 20-rod portage could extend to 25 or 30 rods, and Hog Creek could be a problem. Your 640-rod trek from Kawishiwi Lake to Hog Creek follows a good gravel road; but then, 2 miles is a long portage on any path! Watch for moose in this area; they abound, in spite of the summer influx of canoeists. A road sign marks the Hog Creek access, and a small parking lot is located on the east side of the road just north of the creek. Hog Creek is barely wide enough for a canoe to slip between its brushy banks, and so provides a real challenge for the motor boats that invade it. In addition to the 15-rod portage near the road, small beaver dams may spring up occasionally and require quick liftovers.

DAY 7: **Perent Lake,** p. 61 rods, **Perent River,** p. 31 rods, **river,** p. 25 rods, **river,** p. 33 rods, **river, rapids, river,** p. 17 rods, **river,** p. 39 rods, **river, rapids, river,** p. 22 rods, **river,** p. 16 rods, **river,** p. 40 rods, **river,** 22 rods, **river,** p. 16 rods, **river, Boga Lake,** p. 26 rods, **Isabella Lake,** p. 28 rods, **Isabella River,** p. 15 rods, **river, Island River,** p. 10 rods, **river,** p. 11 rods, **river.** Both Perent and Isabella lakes are easily accessible to motor boats and canoeists, but it seems that few travel between them on the Perent River. Consequently, this final day of your trip will take you through one of the most exciting wilderness experiences in the BWCA, where you will portage between towering virgin pine, stepping on terrain only recently vacated by moose, and over which bald eagles are frequently sighted. (See sketch of the Perent River region below). If you prefer, you may eliminate the final three portages and about three miles of paddling by walking from the public landing on Isabella Lake to your vehicle at the Island River access.

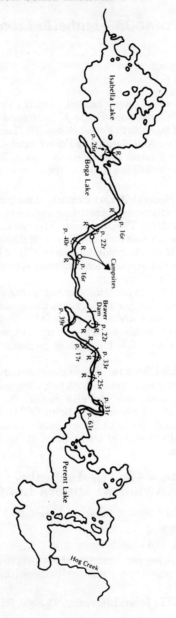

The Perent River

Isabella Lake

Boga Lake

R

p. 26r

R

p. 16r

R

p. 22r

R   R

p. 40r

R

p. 16r

Campsites

Beaver
Dam   p. 22r

R

p. 39r

R   R

R

p. 17r

R   R

p. 33r

R

p. 25r

R

p. 31r

p. 61r

Perent Lake

Hog Creek

Entry Point 35—Isabella Lake

Permits: 386
Popularity Rank: 24
Daily Quota: 4

Location: Isabella Lake is located 28 miles southeast of Ely. To get there, follow Forest Route 172 one mile east from State Highway 1 at Isabella to Forest Route 369. Turn left and follow 369 north for about 6 miles to Forest Route 373, then follow 373 another 6 miles northwest to Forest Route 377. Turn right and follow 377 5½ miles to the public landing at Isabella Lake.

Description: Several Forest Service campgrounds are located along State Highway 1, providing a place to spend the night before your trip. Coming from Ely, you will pass campgrounds at the South Kawishiwi River, McDougal Lakes and Little Isabella River. The closest, however, is at Dumbbell Lake, about 3 miles out of your way, on Forest Route 172, four miles east of Isabella, Minnesota.

Less than half the travel permits for entry into the BWCA through Isabella Lake are issued to groups using canoes without motors. Motor boats are allowed on Isabella Lake, the south half of which is outside of the Boundary Waters. It seems that most of the users of this entry point go no farther than Isabella Lake itself.

You will note that, because of their closeness, the Isabella Lake and Island River entry points both provide good access to canoe routes following the Isabella River. Both routes suggested for the Island River entry point (#34), therefore, could also begin at Isabella Lake. This is good to remember, in case the entry point you wish to use is "filled up" on the day of your scheduled trip.

Route #42: The Isabella-
South Kawishiwi Rivers Loop

5 Days, 57 Miles, 13 Lakes, 3 Rivers, 1 Creek, 37 Portages
Difficulty: Challenging
Fisher maps: 112, 113

Introduction: After the first two short portages, this is exactly the same trip as outlined in Route #40. The only difference is this:

DAY 1: DELETE: **Island River,** p. 11 rods, **River,** p. 10 rods, **river,**

ADD: **Isabella Lake,** p. 28 rods, **Isabella River,** p. 15 rods. The remainder of the route is identical, until you return to the junction of the Island and Isabella rivers. Obviously, you will return to Isabella Lake instead of turning south into the Island River.

Route #43: The Knife Border Route

12 Days, 125 Miles, 46 Lakes, 3 Rivers, 3 Creeks, 78 Portages
Difficulty: Challenging
Fisher maps: 112, 113

Introduction: You'll begin this long route by paddling east across Isabella Lake, through Boga Lake and into one of the most interesting and wildest regions within the BWCA — the Perent River — where you will see virgin pine, bald eagles, and a preponderance of moose. Across Perent Lake and into meandering little Hog Creek, you will then encounter the longest portage of the route — a 2-mile trek on Forest Route 354 to Kawishiwi Lake. From popular Kawishiwi Lake, you will travel north via the scenic lakes and interconnecting creeks that compose the upper reaches of the Kawishiwi River system to Malberg Lake. From Malberg you will angle to the northeast through a less traveled interior part of the BWCA to another popular lake, Little Saganaga, and then north to breathtaking Gabimichigami Lake. You will paddle northwest from Gabi through one of the most beautiful parts of all the Boundary Waters to ever-popular Ogishkemuncie Lake, and then on to the international border at Knife Lake. From the southwest end of sparkling Knife Lake you will portage a weary ⅔ mile to Vera Lake and another ½ mile to Ensign Lake. Your course will then take you southeast through a series of small lakes and short carries to Thomas Lake, and then south to sprawling Lake Insula. Paddling west again, you'll navigate the busy motor route from the southwest end of Lake Insula to the numbered lakes as you return to the Kawishiwi River system. At the southwest end of Lake Two you will portage south into a much less traveled part of the BWCA, from Rock Island Lake to Bald Eagle Lake. Finally, you will paddle east up the lovely Isabella River to your origin at Isabella Lake.

Fishing is usually excellent throughout most of this loop. Walleye and northern pike, in particular, are plentiful in Isabella, Perent, Polly, Koma, Malberg, Kivaniva and Fraser lakes, as well as in most parts of the Kawishiwi River system. Lake trout may also be caught in Little Saganaga,

Gabimichigami, Eddy, Knife and Thomas lakes. In addition, crappies and bass may be found in several of the lakes en route.

About half of this route is open to motor traffic, and the region from Knife Lake south and east to Lake Two, in particular, is quite heavily traveled much of the summer. The Kawishiwi-Polly-Malberg chain of lakes is also very popular, but motorized craft are not allowed there.

The astute wildlife observer will see evidence of beaver throughout the trip, and moose are common in the region between Kawishiwi Lake and Little Saganaga, as well as along the Isabella and Perent rivers.

A good blend of lakes with rivers and small creeks eliminates any chance of boredom along this beautiful route. Although portages are frequent, most are quite short and easily traversed. The longest, however, is 2 miles.

Allow 12 full days to complete this challenging route. 13 would permit more time to fish, however, and 14 would be better for an easy-going crew. Low water and occasional beaver dams could slow travel on the Perent River and Hog Creek.

DAY 1: **Isabella Lake,** p. 26 rods, **Boga Lake,** p. 16 rods, **Perent River,** p. 22 rods, **river,** p. 40 rods, **river,** p. 16 rods, **river,** p. 22 rods, **river, rapids, river,** p. 39 rods, **river,** p. 17 rods, **river, rapids, river,** p. 33 rods, **river,** p. 25 rods, **river,** p. 31 rods, **river,** p. 61 rods, **Perent Lake.** This day will find you in one of the wildest portions of the Boundary Waters, an area containing a very high density moose population. Although both Isabella and Perent lakes are easily accessible to motor boats and canoeists, it seems that few navigate the winding little river between. (See detailed sketch of the Perent River region in Route #41.)

DAY 2: **Perent Lake, Hog Creek,** p. 15 rods, **creek,** p. 640 rods, **Kawishiwi Lake, Kawishiwi River, Square Lake,** p. 20 rods, **Kawishiwi River,** p. 11 rods, **river, Kawasaschong Lake.** Although the southeast end of Perent Lake is not shown on Fisher map #113, you will have no trouble finding the mouth of Hog Creek. (See detailed sketch of the Perent River region in Route #41.) Because of considerable meandering and an opposing current, travel up Hog Creek is slow. In addition to the portage near the creek's junction with Forest Route 354, there may also be occasional beaver dams that require liftovers. Your 2-mile trek is along a good gravel road, but is a burden, nevertheless. When the water level is low, you may run into difficulty in Hog Creek

and in the upper reaches of the Kawishiwi River between
Kawishiwi Lake and Kawasaschong. In fact, the 20-rod portage could be closer to 25 or 30 rods and muddy at the east end.

   DAY 3: **Kawasaschong Lake,** p. 181 rods, **Townline
Lake,** p. 91 rods, **Lake Polly,** p. 19 rods, **Kawishiwi River,** p.
48 rods, **river,** p. 127 rods, **Koma Lake,** p. 24 rods, **Malberg
Lake.** Don't worry about the 181-rod portage between
Kawasaschong and Townline lakes; it is an easy, slightly
downhill trek. You may find fishing for walleye and northern
pike to be excellent in Malberg Lake. Since Malberg is the
apparent destination of many fishermen using this popular
route, you should get a campsite as soon as possible. There are
several very nice ones from which to choose.

   DAY 4: **Malberg Lake,** p. 48 rods, **Kawishiwi River,** p.
40 rods, **Kivaniva Lake,** p. 14-35 rods, **lake,** p. 25 rods, **pond,**
p. 19 rods, **Pan Lake,** p. 55 rods, **pond,** p. 89 rods, **pond,** p. 65
rods, **Makwa Lake,** p. 45 rods, **Elton Lake,** p. 19 rods, **pond,**
p. 19 rods, **Little Saganaga Lake.** None of the portages this
day is difficult, but their frequency will slow travel somewhat.
You will not see as many people between Malberg and Little
Saganaga as on either side of this section of the route. Little
Saganaga Lake itself, however, is quite popular and many of
the campsites there may be taken if you arrive late in the day.
If time permits, you may wish to proceed to one of the pleasant
campsites on the southeast shore of awesome Gabimichigami
Lake. Most of these sites are outstanding for any size of group,
and the view is breathtaking from those that border the main
body of the lake.

   DAY 5: **Little Saganaga Lake,** p. 30 rods, **Rattle Lake,**
p. 25 rods, **Gabimichigami Lake,** p. 15 rods, **Agamok Lake,**
3 portages, **Mueller Lake,** p. 80 rods, **Ogishkemuncie Lake,**
p. 15 rods, **Annie Lake,** p. 15 rods, **Jean Lake,** p. 15 rods,
Eddy Lake, p. 25 rods, **Knife Lake.** On this day you will find
yourself canoeing through some of the most scenic terrain in
all the BWCA. Each part of the route offers a unique form of
beauty, from island-studded Little Saganaga and
Ogishkemuncie lakes to the large, open expanses on
Gabimichigami and Knife lakes to the scenic series of serene
little pools and rapids between Gabi and Ogishkemuncie
lakes. At the northwest end of Agamok Lake you will have a
choice of portages: either three short portages around three
sets of rapids, or one continuous portage of about 100 rods from
Agamok directly to Mueller Lake. If time is of the essence,
choose the latter, but you would not regret taking the time for
the other alternative. All three portages are rocky and some-

what steep in places; but none exceeds 25 rods. The second portage crosses the Kekekabic Trail, which utilizes a wooden bridge to pass over a picturesque waterfall flowing parallel to the portage. Those who bypass the area via the longer portage are missing a real treat!

The 80-rod portage from Mueller into Ogishkemuncie Lake looks innocent on the map, but it's not. It begins with a steep uphill climb, before descending to the lower Ogishkemuncie Lake. Several portage rests along the way will be a welcome relief if you find yourself out of shape.

Ogishkemuncie is a pretty lake and, consequently, quite popular among canoeists originating their trips from both the Gunflint Trail and the Fernberg Road. Knife Lake is also well traveled, and since it constitutes a part of the international boundary, motors are allowed on it. Find a campsite in the South Arm, as camper congestion is common in the southwest end of this very clear lake.

DAY 6: **Knife Lake,** p. 200 rods, **Vera Lake.** This will be a relatively easy day, but your only portage is rough. It begins with a steep climb to an elevation of 80 feet above Knife Lake, follows a ridge for over ½ mile, and then rapidly descends to Vera Lake. Be sure to stop at Dorthy Molter's Isle of Pines in the southwest end of Knife Lake. Dorthy sells home-made root beer to passing canoeists and is a pleasure to visit with. She has lived on her three little islands for over 40 years, in spite of persistent bureaucratic attempts to make her leave her home. Bears are notorious in the vicinity of Vera Lake, so be sure to hang your food pack up well.

DAY 7: **Vera Lake,** p. 180 rods, **Ensign Lake,** p. 53 rods, **Ashigan Lake,** p. 105 rods, **Gibson Lake,** p. 25 rods, **Cattyman Lake,** p. 55 rods, **Jordan Lake,** p. 5 rods, **Ima Lake.** You will be doing a lot of uphill walking this day. After the first long downhill carry, the remaining five are all uphill, including steep climbs from Ensign to Ashigan Lake and from Gibson to Cattyman Lake. You'll find many good campsites on Ima Lake.

DAY 8: **Ima Lake,** p. 50 rods, **Hatchet Lake,** p. 10 rods, **creek,** p. 10 rods, **creek,** p. 10 rods, **pond,** p. 5 rods, **Thomas Lake,** p. 25 rods, **Kiana Lake,** p. 179 rods, **Lake Insula.** If the water level is high enough, you may be able to eliminate the first two 10-rod portages between Hatchet and Thomas lakes by pulling your canoe up the shallow rapids. On the other hand, if the water level is quite low, you may find it necessary to walk your canoe through portions of the shallow creek, in addition to taking all three 10-rod portages. The ½-mile carry from Kiana to Lake Insula is mostly downhill.

DAY 9: **Lake Insula,** p. 105 rods, **Hudson Lake, Kawishiwi River,** p. 10 rods, **river,** p. 25 rods, **river,** p. 20 rods, **Lake Four, Lake Three, Lake Two.** You will see more and more canoes the farther west you get this day, and motors are not an uncommon sound. Find a campsite early, before they are all taken. If time permits, you may wish to continue on to Clearwater Lake, a peaceful and pretty lake that few people visit.

DAY 10: **Lake Two,** p. 65 rods, **Rock Island Lake,** p. 242 rods, **Clearwater Lake,** p. 125 rods, **Camdre Lake,** p. 64 rods, **Pietro Lake,** p. 50 rods, **Gull Lake,** p. 41 rods, **Gull Creek,** p. 189 rods, **Bald Eagle Lake.** Your first three portages are generally uphill, while the last four are downhill. None is difficult, including the 242-rod path to Clearwater Lake, which follows a nearly level course most of the way. The campsites at the northwest end of Bald Eagle Lake are more attractive than those at the southeast end, but you will have to paddle out of your way on this wide-open lake to enjoy the better ones.

DAY 11: **Bald Eagle Lake,** p. 190 rods, **Isabella River, rapids, river,** p. 40 rods, **river,** p. 40 rods, **river,** p. 27 rods, **river,** p. 27 rods, **river,** p. 10 rods, **river, Rice Lake.** You can probably eliminate the final 10-rod portage before Rice Lake by pulling your canoe up the short rapids there. Watch for moose along the banks of this scenic river. If you arrive at Rice Lake early in the afternoon, you will have plenty of time to continue on to Isabella Lake and conclude this trip — but that makes a long day for the average group.

DAY 12: **Rice Lake, Isabella River,** p. 130 rods, **river,** p. 15 rods, **river,** p. 28 rods, **Isabella Lake.** Make sure you bear left at the junction of the Isabella and Island rivers, just before the 15-rod portage. You should have no trouble making it back to your origin at Forest Route 377 by noon.

Entry Point 36—Hog Creek

Permits: 259
Popularity Rank: 33
Daily Quota: 5

Location: Hog Creek is located about 35 miles southeast of Ely, midway between Ely and the Gunflint Trail, accessible from the Sawbill Trail to the east as well as from Highway 1. From Highway 1 at Isabella, follow Forest Route 172 east for 12 miles to County Road 7. Turn left and follow 7 north for 11 miles to the junction with Forest Route 354. Then go 2 miles north on 354 to Hog Creek.

Description: Unlike its neighbor entry point, Kawishiwi Lake, Hog Creek attracts few canoeists to its winding wilderness. Because it is a designated motor route into Perent Lake, motor boats are more common than canoes without motors. In fact, only 38% of the use permits issued during 1977 went to groups using canoes without motors. As a result, most of the travel through this entry point goest no farther than Perent Lake, leaving the Perent River to the few canoeists who avail themselves of this fascinating stream. Consequently, this area is still one of the wildest sections within the BWCA, containing a high density of moose and permitting frequent sightings of bald eagles.

A nice public campground is located 2 miles north of Hog Creek on Forest Route 354, adjacent to the Kawishiwi Lake access. There are only a few campsites, however, so plan to arrive early if you wish to spend the night there before your departure into the Boundary Waters Canoe Area.

Route #44: "Three Rivers" Route

7 Days, 88 Miles, 20 Lakes, 3 Rivers, 1 Creek, 50 Portages
Difficulty: Challenging
Fisher maps: 112, 113

Introduction: This fascinating route follows nearly the same course as the Four Rivers Route (#41) — minus the Island River. It will take you west from Forest Route 354, down the narrow meandering channel of Hog Creek, across Perent Lake and into the pristine wilderness of the Perent River, across Isabella Lake and on down the lovely Isabella River to the base of Bald Eagle Lake. From there you'll point northwest and navigate the open waters of Bald Eagle and Gabbro until you intersect the South Kawishiwi River. Up the beautiful pools and rapids of the Kawishiwi River, you'll paddle, pull and carry your canoe, north and east across the popular "numbered lakes" and island-studded Lake Insula. On up the Kawishiwi River you will pause to view a display of ancient Indian pictographs decorating the vertical cliffs along its shore. At Malberg Lake you'll turn south and continue on up the system of lakes, ponds and creeks that compose the upper reaches of the Kawishiwi, until you reach its source at Kawishiwi Lake. From there, a two-mile trek on Forest Route 354 will return you to your origin at the Hog Creek Entry Point. (See Introduction, Route #41.)

DAY 1: **Hog Creek,** p. 15 rods, **creek, Perent Lake,** p. 61 rods, **Perent River,** p. 31 rods, **river,** p. 25 rods, **river,** p. 33 rods, **river, rapids, river,** p. 17 rods, **river,** p. 39 rods, **river, rapids, river,** p. 22 rods, **river,** p. 16 rods, **river,** p. 40 rods, **river,** p. 22 rods, **river,** p. 16 rods, **river, Boga Lake,** p. 26 rods, **Isabella Lake.** (See comments for Days 6 and 7, Route #41.)

DAY 2: **Isabella Lake,** p. 28 rods, **Isabella River,** p. 15 rods, **river,** p. 130 rods, **river, Rice Lake, Isabella River,** p. 10 rods, **river,** p. 27 rods, **river,** p. 27 rods, **river,** p. 40 rods, **river,** p. 40 rods, **river, rapids, river,** p. 190 rods, **Bald Eagle Lake.** (See comments for Day 1, Route #40.)

DAY 3: **Bald Eagle Lake, rapids, Gabbro Lake, Little Gabbro Lake,** p. 122 rods, **South Kawishiwi River,** p. 28 rods, **river,** p. 18 rods, **river,** p. 12 rods, **river, Kawishiwi River,** p. 8 rods, **river,** p. 40 rods, **river,** p. 20 rods, **river,** p. 19 rods, **Lake One.** (See comments for Day 2, Route #41.)

DAY 4: **Lake One,** p. 30 rods, **pond,** p. 45 rods, **Lake Two, Lake Three, Lake Four,** p. 20 rods, **Kawishiwi River,** p. 25 rods, **river,** p. 10 rods, **river, Hudson Lake.** (See comments for Day 3, Route #41.)

DAY 5: **Hudson Lake,** p. 105 rods, **Lake Insula,** p. 18 rods, **Kawishiwi River, Alice Lake,** p. 20 rods, **Kawishiwi River,** p. 90 rods, **Kawishiwi River,** p. 15 rods, **river.** (See comments for Day 4, Route #41.)

DAY 6: **Kawishiwi River,** p. 60 rods, **Malberg Lake,** p. 24 rods, **Koma Lake,** p. 127 rods, **Kawishiwi River,** p. 48 rods, **river,** p. 19 rods, **Lake Polly,** p. 91 rods, **Townline Lake,** p. 181 rods, **Kawasaschong Lake.** (See comments for Day 5, Route #41.)

DAY 7: **Kawasaschong Lake, Kawishiwi River,** p. 11 rods, **river,** p. 20 rods, **Square Lake, Kawishiwi River, Kawishiwi Lake, Forest Route 354 to Hog Creek.** When the water level is low, the 20-rod portage could extend to 25 or

30 rods. Keep an eye out for moose; they are thick in this area, in spite of the summer influx of canoeists. Unless you have made prior arrangements to have your vehicle waiting at the Kawishiwi Lake access, the final two miles of your trip will have to be on foot.

Entry Point 37—Kawishiwi Lake

Permits: 653
Popularity Rank: 17
Daily Quota: 8

Location: Kawishiwi Lake is located about 35 miles southeast of Ely. From Highway 1 at Isabella, follow Forest Route 172 east for 12 miles to County Road 7. Turn left and follow 7 north for 11 miles to the junction with Forest Route 354. Kawishiwi Lake is at the north end of Route 354, 4 miles from County Road 7. It is also accessible from the Sawbill Trail to the east.

Description: In spite of its remote location, about midway between Ely and Lake Superior, the Kawishiwi Lake entry point is quite popular among canoeists. There are nearly 50 designated Forest Service campsites from Kawishiwi to Malberg Lake to accommodate the use. And much of the traffic goes no further than Malberg. In spite of the heavy use, moose are not an uncommon sight throughout the area. I have seen them beside Square Lake in mid-afternoon, and drinking from Malberg Lake in the early morning.

A nice public campground adjacent to the Kawishiwi access provides a good spot to spend the night before your trip into the Boundary Waters. There are only a few campsites, however, so plan to arrive early, and avoid the busier weekends.

Route #45: The "Gabi-Gishke-Kabic" Loop

6 Days, 68 Miles, 34 Lakes, 1 River, 1 Creek, 56 Portages
Difficulty: Rugged
Fisher map: 113

Introduction: This portage-laden route will lead you north through the lakes and streams of the upper Kawishiwi River system to the fishing paradise on Malberg Lake. From Malberg you'll angle to the northeast through the seldom-traveled interior of the Boundary Waters to popular Little Saganaga Lake, and north to breathtaking Gabimichigami Lake. You'll exit "Gabi" to the northwest, cross the famous Kekekabic Trail and visit the ever-popular Ogishkemuncie Lake. Eight portages to the west, you'll welcome the inspirational sight of big Kekekabic Lake, bordered with beautiful, towering bluffs, and surrounded by hills rising as high as

400 feet above the water. You will portage out of "Kek" to the south and soon re-enter the part of the BWCA that is seldom penetrated by the casual canoeist, before returning to Malberg Lake and retracing your path back to Kawishiwi Lake.

Motors are banned from the entire loop. Although the southern and northern sections are heavily used, you'll find an adequate degree of solitude in the central portion, north of Malberg Lake. Some of the most spectacular scenery in the central region of the BWCA will be viewed along this route. And even though portaging is all too frequent, only five carries exceed 100 rods.

This is a good route for the wildlife enthusiast. Evidence of beaver will be found all along the way, and moose are not uncommon, especially in the region south of Little Saganaga to Kawishiwi Lake.

Walleye and northern pike fishing may be excellent in Polly, Koma, Malberg, Kivaniva and Fraser lakes. Lake trout may also be caught in Little Saganaga, Gabimichigami, Eddy and Kekekabic lakes. A fishing rod and license are a must for this trip. Although an experienced group of strong canoeists could easily complete this route in 5 days or less, I suggest 6 for the "average" voyageurs.

DAY 1: **Kawishiwi Lake, Kawishiwi River, Square Lake,** p. 20 rods, **Kawishiwi River,** p. 11 rods, **river, Kawasaschong Lake,** p. 181 rods, **Townline Lake,** p. 91 rods, **Lake Polly,** p. 19 rods, **Kawishiwi River,** p. 48 rods, **river,** p. 127 rods, **Koma Lake,** p. 24 rods, **Malberg Lake.** Your first day will take you through the lovely small lakes and streams that compose the upper part of the Kawishiwi River system. The portages are fairly well scattered throughout the day and not difficult. Even the 181-rod portage leading from Kawasaschong Lake is an easy, slightly downhill trek. Campsites are plentiful from Lake Polly to Malberg Lake. Since Malberg is the apparent destination of many fishermen using this popular route, however, you might be wise to stop on Koma. The 20-rod portage on the river between Square and Kawasaschong lakes may be as long as 25-30 rods when the water level is low. Keep your eyes open for moose in this area.

DAY 2: **Malberg Lake,** p. 48 rods, **Kawishiwi River,** p. 40 rods, **Kivaniva Lake,** p. 14-35 rods, **lake,** p. 25 rods, **pond,** p. 19 rods, **Pan Lake,** p. 55 rods, **pond,** p. 89 rods, **pond,** p. 65 rods, **Makwa Lake,** p. 45 rods, **Elton Lake,** p. 19 rods, **pond,** p. 19 rods, **Little Saganaga Lake.** None of the portages this day is difficult, but their frequency will slow travel somewhat. You won't see as many people between Malberg and Little

Saganaga as north or south of this section of the route. However, Little Saganaga Lake itself is quite popular, and many of the campsites here may be taken if you arrive late in the day. If time permits, you may wish to proceed to one of the pleasant campsites on the southeast shore of awesome Gabimichigami Lake. Most of these sites are outstanding for any size of group, and the view is breathtaking from those that border the main body of the lake.

DAY 3: **Little Saganaga Lake,** p. 30 rods, **Rattle Lake,** p. 25 rods, **Gabimichigami Lake,** p. 15 rods, **Agamok Lake,** 3 portages, **Mueller Lake,** p. 80 rods, **Ogishkemuncie Lake,** p. 15 rods, **Annie Lake,** p. 15 rods, **Jean Lake,** p. 15 rods, **Eddy Lake,** 5 portages, **Kekekabic Lake.** On this day you will find yourself canoeing through some of the most scenic terrain in all the BWCA. Each part of the route offers a unique form of beauty, from island-studded Little Saganaga and Ogishkemuncie lakes, to the large open expanses of Gabimichigami and Kekekabic lakes, to the serene little ponds between Eddy and Kekekabic lakes. A favorite section of mine is between Gabimichigami and Ogishkemuncie. Agamok is more like a river than a lake, connecting Gabi with a series of ponds and rapids that flow into Mueller Lake. Here you have a choice: either three short portages around three sets of rapids, or one continuous portage of about 100 rods from Agamok directly to Mueller. If time is of the essence, choose the latter. But you will not regret taking the time for the other alternative. All three portages are rocky and somewhat steep in places, but none exceeds 25 rods. The second portage crosses the Kekekabic Trail, which utilizes a wooden bridge to pass over a picturesque waterfall flowing parallel to the portage. Those who bypass the area via the longer portage are missing a real treat.

The 80-rod portage from Mueller into Ogishkemuncie Lake looks innocent on the map, but it's not. It makes a steep uphill climb before descending to lower Ogishkemuncie Lake. Several canoe rests along the way will be a welcome relief if you find that you are not in as good shape as you had thought.

Ogishkemuncie is a pretty lake and, consequently, quite popular among canoeists beginning their trip from the Gunflint Trail or the Fernberg Road. So is Kekekabic Lake, which is more difficult to reach, but well worth the effort. The five short portages into the Kekekabic ponds are barely more than "liftovers." Though neither long nor difficult, they are a nuisance at the end of a day already filled with portages.

Few other experiences will awaken your feeling that you

have discovered Paradise more than entering Kekekabic Lake from the east after a long, hard day. As you leave the last of the five portages from the ponds, the narrow entrance to the lake will gradually widen as it winds to the west. The evening sun hovering over the far-distant shoreline accentuates the high-rising bluffs that encircle this magnificent lake. And in the distance, you'll see hills rising as high as 400 feet. Several campsites are located near the east end of the lake, and you would be wise to grab the first one you see, because Kekekabic attracts many visitors. A trail leading from the south shore of the lake (one mile from the east end) will take you to a fire-watch tower about a half-mile hike up from the shoreline. There you'll find an incredible view of the surrounding countryside.

DAY 4: **Kekekabic Lake**, p. 85 rods, **Strup Lake**, p. 10 rods, **Wisini Lake**, p. 90 rods, **Ahmakose Lake**, p. 30 rods, **Gerund Lake**, p. 15 rods, **Fraser Lake**, p. 65 rods, **Sagus Lake**, p. 42 rods, **Roe Lake**, p. 60 rods, **Cap Lake**, p. 220 rods, **Boulder Lake**. You'll find three campsites from which to choose on Boulder Lake, without much competition for them. This is in one of the least traveled parts of the Boundary Waters, and here you will more than likely find the solitude that you desire. The five portages between Kekekabic Lake and Fraser don't appear as much on the map, but don't underestimate them! The 85-rod portage out of Kekekabic climbs over 100 feet before descending 21 feet to Strup Lake. The next short portage ascends 17 feet in its 10-rod length. And, although Wisini and Ahmakose lakes lie at nearly the same elevation, the 90-rod portage climbs 54 feet above them. But after that it's all downhill. The 220-rod portage from Cap into Boulder is the longest of the trip, but level. As you approach the east end of Cap Lake, you will see two portages leading into the woods. The one on the left leads to Ledge Lake; the right one leads to Boulder Lake. After walking 85 rods toward Boulder Lake, you'll come to a split in the trail. Be sure you take the *right* trail here, or you may find yourself on Ledge Lake, 280 long rods from your target.

DAY 5: **Boulder Lake, liftover, creek,** p. 15 rods, **creek, Adams Lake,** p. 90 rods, **Elbow Lake,** p. 30 rods, **pond,** p. 15 rods, **Kawishiwi River,** p. 60 rods, **Malberg Lake,** p. 24 rods, **Koma Lake,** p. 127 rods, **Kawishiwi River,** p. 48 rods, **river,** p. 19 rods, **Lake Polly.** Your fifth day will bring you out of the more isolated interior of the BWCA and back to the more heavily used Kawishiwi River system feeding Malberg Lake. There are many good campsites on Lake Polly, but once again there are many more people with whom to compete. Take advantage of the fine fishing available in Polly, Koma and Malberg, where walleye and northern pike abound, and try to make camp early this day.

Low water may seriously hinder navigation of the creek between Boulder and Adams lakes. Beaver dams may also interfere. But under normal conditions you should be able to paddle all but about 15 rods of this half-mile stream.

DAY 6: **Lake Polly,** p. 91 rods, **Townline Lake,** p. 181 rods, **Kawasaschong Lake, Kawishiwi River,** p. 11 rods, **river,** p. 20 rods, **Square Lake, Kawishiwi River, Kawishiwi Lake.** This is, of course, familiar territory to you now. This final part of your trip could be completed on the fifth day, but the pressure would no doubt detract from your enjoyment of this pretty route.

Route #46: Three Rivers Route

8 Days, 88 Miles, 21 Lakes, 3 Rivers, 1 Creek, 51 Portages
Difficulty: Challenging
Fisher maps: 112, 113

Introduction: This delightful route will take you north from Kawishiwi Lake through the lakes, streams, pools and rapids that compose the Kawishiwi River system. From Malberg Lake you'll head southwest down the Kawishiwi River, taking time out to view ancient Indian pictographs along its shore, through Lake Insula and the "numbered lakes" chain to the South Kawishiwi River. Here, you'll have an opportunity to shoot rapids. Turning southeast, you'll encounter the greatest amount of "open water" on Gabbro and Bald Eagle lakes. From there you will portage into the Isabella River and paddle up this beautiful stream to Isabella Lake. Continuing east, you'll soon enter one of the wildest and most interesting regions within the BWCA — the Perent River, where you will portage between towering virgin pines, stepping on terrain only recently vacated by moose and sighting bald eagles overhead. Across Perent Lake and through the winding wilderness of Hog Creek, you will return to Forest Route 354, just 2 miles south of your origin.

Wildlife abounds in this region. Beaver homes abound along the Kawishiwi River and moose are also a common sight, especially in the region through which flow the Isabella and Perent rivers. My wife and I saw eight moose along this route during the Summer of 1977, and we're not among the quietest of paddlers. So, with a little effort, you can hardly miss!

Fishing is generally excellent throughout the loop. Wall-eye and northern pike, in particular, are plentiful in Perent and Isabella lakes, in all parts of the Kawishiwi River and in Malberg, Koma and Polly lakes. Crappies and bass can also be found in several of the lakes.

About half of the route is open to motor traffic, and the region around Lake One, in particular, is quite heavily used during much of the summer. The Kawishiwi-Polly-Malberg chain of lakes is also very popular. But the variety of beauty that exists along the Three Rivers Route more than compensates for the number of people encountered along the way. A good blend of lakes with rivers and small creeks eliminates any chance of boredom. And although portages are frequent, most are quite short and easily traversed: the longest is 190 rods.

Allow eight full days to complete this challenging route. Nine would permit more time to fish. Low water and occasional beaver dams may slow travel considerably, especially on the Perent River and Hog Creek, as well as eliminate the possibility of running rapids on the South Kawishiwi River. An efficient crew of experienced canoeists could complete the route in seven days, or even less.

DAY 1: **Kawishiwi Lake, Kawishiwi River, Square Lake,** p. 20 rods, **Kawishiwi River,** p. 11 rods, **river, Kawasaschong Lake,** p. 181 rods, **Townline Lake,** p. 91 rods, **Lake Polly,** p. 19 rods, **Kawishiwi River,** p. 48 rods, **river,** p. 127 rods, **Koma Lake.** (See comments for Day 1, Route #45.)

DAY 2: **Koma Lake,** p. 24 rods, **Malberg Lake,** p. 60 rods, **Kawishiwi River,** p. 15 rods, **river,** p. 90 rods, **river,** p. 20 rods, **Alice Lake, Kawishiwi River,** p. 18 rods, **Lake Insula.** Fishing for walleye and northern pike may be excellent in Malberg and along the Kawishiwi River, as well as in Lake Insula. Take time to make a short side trip to the Indian pictographs, just south of the 90-rod portage approaching Alice Lake. A careful examination of the vertical cliffs bordering the river on the west side will yield reminders of a civilization that once flourished in this water wilderness.

DAY 3: **Lake Insula,** p. 105 rods, **Hudson Lake, Kawishiwi River,** p. 10 rods, **river,** p. 25 rods, **river,** p. 20 rods, **Lake Four, Lake Three, Lake Two,** p. 45 rods, **pond,** p. 30 rods, **Lake One.** You will be traveling the entire day on a heavily used motor route as you approach the sixth most popular entry point into the BWCA — Lake One. Island-studded Lake Insula is beautiful, but may provide a challenge to the novice map reader. You would do well to plan your trip so that you do not arrive at Lake One on Saturday, Sunday or Monday, when campsites may be at a premium. If supplies are in need of replenishing, a brief stop may be in order at Kawishiwi Lodge, located just outside the BWCA on the northern tip of Lake One.

DAY 4: **Lake One,** p. 19 rods, **Kawishiwi River,** p. 20 rods, **river,** p. 40 rods, **river,** p. 8 rods, **river, South Kawishiwi River,** p. 12 rods, **river,** p. 18 rods, **river,** p. 28 rods, **river,** p. 122 rods, **Little Gabbro Lake, Gabbro Lake.** If desired, you may bypass the "civilized" northern part of Lake One, where the Kawishiwi Lodge and the public landing are located, by portaging 41 rods into Confusion Lake and then 25 rods back into the Kawishiwi River. This eliminates about three miles of paddling, but increases portaging by 47 rods. For those who prefer a little white water to the drudgery of a portage, four of the six portages on the Kawishiwi River this day can be avoided (20, 12, 18 and 28 rods) by shooting, lining or walking the respective rapids, depending on the water depth. Be sure to check them out first, however, because, although the rapids are not considered dangerous, sharp rocks could damage your canoe. The true adventurer with time to kill can also avoid the 122-rod portage from the South Kawishiwi River to Little Gabbro Lake by walking up two sets of gentle rapids, and portaging a small waterfall and an old logging dam. The map won't show this, so here is what to look for: Just beyond the 122-rod portage you'll encounter a short stretch of rapids that must be walked up (no portage). Bearing to the left shoreline, you'll soon come to a picturesque little waterfall that must be passed on the left by a steep, overgrown 10-rod portage that appears to have been used only once or twice since the last Chippewa Indians moved out of the region. Soon after, you will again have to walk up a somewhat longer stretch of rapids, until you arrive at the old dam, which can be passed on the right via an even less traveled path. *Voila:* the back door to Little Gabbro Lake. It is kind of fun, but takes much longer than the 122-rod portage.

DAY 5: **Gabbro Lake,** p. 2-5 rods, **Bald Eagle Lake,** p. 190 rods, **Isabella River, rapids, river,** p. 40 rods, **river,** p. 40 rods, **river.** A small but swift rapids separates Gabbro and Bald Eagle lakes. Your canoe could be pulled through it, if you prefer to avoid the short but tricky portage on the right.

Fishing is good here, below the rapids. The Isabella is an attractive river, along which moose may be seen. But campsites are few, and none are large enough to adequately accommodate a large group. If necessary, you can leave the Isabella River for the night by portaging 99 rods to Quadga Lake, where three Forest Service campsites are located. Although this day may appear short on a map, remember that you will be traveling upstream and meandering considerably. It is longer than it looks.

DAY 6: **Isabella River,** p. 27 rods, **river,** p. 27 rods, **river,** p. 10 rods, **river, Rice Lake, Isabella River,** p. 130 rods, **river,** p. 15 rods, **river,** p. 28 rods, **Isabella Lake.** You can avoid the 10-rod portage before Rice Lake by pulling your canoe up this short rapids. Be sure to bear left as you pass the junction of the Island River with the Isabella River. Several good campsites are located on Isabella Lake. The southern shore is outside of the BWCA and is accessible via Forest Route 377, so motors may be seen and heard here.

DAY 7: **Isabella Lake,** p. 26 rods, **Boga Lake,** p. 16 rods, **Perent River,** p. 22 rods, **river,** p. 40 rods, **river,** p. 16 rods, **river,** p. 22 rods, **river, rapids, river,** p. 39 rods, **river,** p. 17 rods, **river, rapids, river,** p. 33 rods, **river,** p. 25 rods, **river,** p. 31 rods, **river,** p. 61 rods, **Perent Lake.** This day will find you in one of the wildest parts of the Boundary Waters, an area containing a high moose population. Although both Isabella and Perent lakes are easily accessible to motor boats and canoeists, it seems that few navigate the winding river between. (See detailed sketch of the Perent River region in Route #41.)

DAY 8: **Perent Lake, Hog Creek,** p. 15 rods, **creek, Forest Route 354.** This final leg of your trip could be completed on the seventh day. But be sure to allow enough time to negotiate the meandering path of Hog Creek. And, unless you have made prior arrangements to have a vehicle at the intersection of Hog Creek with Forest Route 354, you will have to walk the last 2 miles to your origin on Kawishiwi Lake.

The southeast corner of Perent Lake and the mouth of Hog Creek are not shown on Fisher map #113. The creek is not difficult to find, however. While paddling southeast past the point at which the map ends, stay along the left shoreline and you will find the entrance to Hog Creek just past a small bay in which a campsite is located. (See detailed sketch of Perent River region in Route #41.)

Appendix I
Routes Categorized by Difficulty and Duration

Duration	Route #	Entry-Point Name (and #)
Easy Trips		
3 days	#31	Wood Lake (#26)
3 days	#33	Snowbank Lake (#27)
5 days	#25	Range River (#23)
5 days	#28	Fall Lake (#24)
Challenging Routes		
3 days	#35	Lake One (#30)
3 days	#38	South Kawishiwi River (#32)
4 days	#23	Horse Lake (#22)
4 days	#27	Fall Lake (#24)
4 days	#29	Moose Lake (#25)
4 days	#32	Wood Lake (#26)
4 days	#37	Farm Lake (#31)
5 days	#36	Lake One (#30)
5 days	#39	South Kawishiwi River (#32)
5 days	#40	Island River (#34)
5 days	#42	Isabella Lake (#35)
6 days	#15	Little Indian Sioux River (#14)
7 days	#13	Little Vermilion Lake (#12)
7 days	#22	Fourtown Lake (#21)
7 days	#34	Snowbank Lake (#27)
7 days	#41	Island River (#34)
12 days	#43	Isabella Lake (#35)
7 days	#44	Hog Creek (#36)
8 days	#18	Moose River (#16)
8 days	#26	Range River (#23)
8 days	#30	Moose Lake (#25)
8 days	#46	Kawishiwi Lake (#37)
9 days	#16	Little Indian Sioux River (#14)
9 days	#24	Horse Lake (#22)
10 days	#4	Crab Lake (#4)
12 days	#14	Little Vermilion Lake (#12)
Rugged Expeditions		
3 days	#3	Crab Lake (#4)
3 days	#5	Slim Lake (#6)

3 days	#7	Big Lake (#7)
3 days	#21	Fourtown Lake (#21)
4 days	#1	Trout Lake (#1)
4 days	#9	Big Moose Lake (#8)
4 days	#19	Stuart River (#19)
5 days	#11	Little Indian Sioux River (#9)
5 days	#17	Moose River (#16)
6 days	#8	Big Lake (#7)
6 days	#45	Kawishiwi Lake (#37)
7 days	#2	Trout Lake (#1)
7 days	#6	Slim Lake (#6)
7 days	#20	Stuart River (#19)
8 days	#10	Big Moose Lake (#8)
10 days	#12	Little Indian Sioux River (#9)

Appendix II
1977 BWCA Travel Permit Data

Entry Point # and Name	Rank	Total # permits	Paddle canoe #	% Paddle canoes
Echo Trail Region				
1-Trout Lake	7	1840	118	7%
4-Crab Lake	26	317	301	95%
6-Slim Lake	34	258	185	72%
7-Big Lake	60	34	25	74%
8-Big Moose Lake	62	32	22	69%
9-Indian Sioux River, South	60	34	31	91%
12-Little Vermilion Lake	9	1105	124	11%
14-Indian Sioux River, North	13	779	653	84%
16-Moose River	12	934	775	83%
19-Stuart River	49	92	79	86%
21-Fourtown Lake	28	308	229	74%
22-Horse Lake	35	244	231	95%
23-Range River	8	1312	151	12%
Fernberg Road Region				
24-Fall Lake	3	2992	1493	50%
25-Moose Lake	1	7705	4353	56%
26-Wood Lake	47	105	81	77%
27-Snowbank Lake	11	1003	588	59%
30-Lake One	4	2586	1679	65%
31-Farm Lake	21	516	307	59%
State Highway 1 Region				
32-South Kawishiwi River	30	302	191	63%
34-Island River	43	143	114	80%
35-Isabella Lake	24	386	188	49%
36-Hog Creek	33	259	98	38%
37-Kawishiwi Lake	17	653	622	95%

Rank: With "1" being the most popular entry point, this is based on the total number of travel permits issued for each of the 73 designated BWCA entry points.

Total # Permits: For all modes of travel through each entry point, including paddle canoes, motor canoes, motor boats, hiking, & other.

Paddle Canoe #: # of permits issued to groups using canoes without motors.

% of Paddle Canoes: % of total permits issued to groups using canoes without motors.

Index